Warm Firesides Wide Porches

Remembering the 1940s in an Authentic Southern Town

Sally Ann Webb McPherson

No part of this publication may be reproduced
in whole or in part, or stored in a retrieval system,
or transmitted in any form or by any means,
electronic, mechanical, photocopying, recording,
or otherwise, without written permission of the author,
except for the inclusion of brief quotations in a review.
For information regarding permission, please write to:
info@barringerpublishing.com

Copyright © 2013 Sally Ann Webb McPherson
All rights reserved.

Barringer Publishing, Naples, Florida
www.barringerpublishing.com
Cover, graphics, layout design by Lisa Camp
Editing by Carole Greene

ISBN: 978-0-9891694-3-1

Library of Congress Cataloging-in-Publication Data
Warm Firesides Wide Porches / Sally Ann Webb McPherson

Printed in U.S.A.

Warm Firesides Wide Porches

Dedication

This book is dedicated to my daughter, Margaret McPherson, without whom there would be no book. She researched and did the layout for the family tree. She photographed the many portraits. She carefully restored literally hundreds of faded and wrinkled photographs from the 1940s. As she worked on the photographs she would often call or write me saying, "Mom, write about this." I would, and I enjoyed the remembering and the writing. She enjoyed the stories.

I came to realize that my childhood in the 1940s would be totally foreign to children and many adults living in the 21st Century. I did my best to recreate those times, and using the restored photographs, illustrate the clothes, cars, houses, downtown, historic buildings and town characters.

Being a southerner who enjoys good stories, I also recognized that my remembering has its share of good stories.

Thank you to other family, friends and writers who read the manuscript and provided comments and encouragement.

Preface

Hillsborough, North Carolina is a special place in central Carolina. Here trading routes crossed a river and the Eno and Occoneechee Indians created settlements in rolling southern foothills, amid forests and fields rich in diverse plants and animals.

Settled by immigrant farmers and merchants from Scotland, Ireland and England in the 1700s, Hillsborough remained a center of commerce in colonial times and became one of the colonial capitals of the North Carolina colony. At that time, Hillsborough was home to many of North Carolina's and the nation's prominent families, as well as signers of both the Declaration of Independence and the Constitution. These were innovative, involved people who saw needs and addressed them, who saw opportunities and embraced them, who led and taught and healed and explored. These people ensured not only their own personal future but also the future of North Carolina and of the United States of America.

Exceptional people in an extraordinary place constitute the history of the Hillsborough I knew growing up. Here, oral history abounded and stories and tall tales were told by warm firesides and on wide porches, recalling past times and inspiring the future.

My Hillsborough forefathers were businessmen and planters. They were delegates to important colonial conventions; they were friends of and corresponded regularly with writers and signers of the Declaration of Independence and the Constitution of the United States. They were instrumental in the founding of the University of North Carolina. They were lawyers and judges framing legal concepts and opinions still studied in the 21st century. As medical doctors, they created the first medical societies and they led in medical science. They were ministers of the Anglican Church and the Methodist Church; they were also educators and founders of schools.

My ancestors scouted for John Smith at Jamestown, they married explorers who were the first to traverse the North American continent, and they contracted with Daniel Boone to explore the west.

In the mid-19th century, two of my great-grandfathers who were staunch unionists participated in the Peace Conference in Washington DC in an effort to save the Union. During the Civil war, my great grandfather fighting for the Confederacy was promoted to adjutant-general on the battle field; women defended the home front with courage and zeal; doctors treated the wounded in their homes.

The town of Hillsborough, North Carolina took its name from the Earl of Hillsborough, Wills Hill, who was the British Secretary of State for the American colonies and a relative of the royal governor, Governor William Tryon. By the mid-1800s, the practical, no-frills/no-nonsense settlers had shortened the name to Hillsboro; and so it was in the 1940s when I was a child. In 1965, the name was changed back to its original spelling.

Historical markers, beautiful old churches with interesting graveyards, old homes, a Masonic Lodge, the Colonial Inn and an architecturally significant courthouse stood comfortably surrounded by ancient trees.

This sense of place is significant to the stories you are about to read. If places could talk, the town of Hillsborough, North Carolina would have a lot to say. Here, the author recounts one decade of the town's history through the eyes, ears, voice, thought and heart of a little girl who lived there in the 1940s.

Sally Ann Webb McPherson

A Moment in Time

Growing up in the 1940s in Hillsborough was for me a moment in time, forever in sepia.

I was born in 1939, the daughter of Alice Cooke Webb and Thomas Norfleet Webb, Jr., and I had two brothers—Skippy, who was three years older than I, and Paul Cameron, who was two years younger.

Many people in the South either had a double name or a nickname, or both. When I think of childhood in Hillsborough, I become Sally Ann, and my brother Paul becomes Paul Cameron. Soft southern voices could play those double names like lyrics in a sweet song; or they could string them out into eternity, carefully, deftly and precisely hammering on each syllable to let you know you were in trouble, or about to be in trouble.

My brother Skippy, who was Thomas Norfleet Webb—named for our father and grandfather—missed out on the double-name deal, but he was a victim of the quirky nickname tradition. We also had Gyp, Boo, Grumpy, Possum and Pooh. My daddy had a cousin called Mack; I always thought it was because he had a middle name that was Scotch-Irish. But no, his given name was Henry, and his nickname derived from the fact that he loved macaroni. Even business and professional associates called him Mack.

Paul Cameron got both the double name and the nickname. Grown men around town called him "Hard-Rock." I did not know the word *redundant* at the time, but it seemed kind of repetitive to me. Yet the name did fit somehow. Maybe it was because Paul Cameron seemed double-hardheaded, double-tough and double-unyielding.

My friend Buck Roberts' real name was Bryan. His father was Dr. Francis Marion Roberts, but no one called him Francis or Marion even though Francis Marion was a hero of the American Revolutionary War. Francis Marion was a Southerner and he had a nickname himself: he was called the Swamp Fox. People on a first-name basis with Dr. Roberts called him "Croaker" after an old mule that used to haul freight from the train station to town.

My father's family had been in Hillsborough for generations with Webb ancestors prominent in the settlement of the country, the Revolutionary War, the founding of the University of North Carolina, in medicine, education, law, agriculture, business and government. My family tree includes Webbs, Hoggs and Huskes, Kirklands, Nashes, Ruffins, Bennehans, Camerons, Peebles, Hills, Cheshires, Blounts—all names familiar to North Carolina historians. As a child, I thought I was kin to everybody in North Carolina. With ancestors having families of fourteen children, that might have been possible. At any rate, they were hard to keep track of, especially with girls marrying into families with different names. It seemed like my relatives were all "kissin' cousins" who almost always commented on how much I had grown.

I could not keep all the cousins straight and never did understand how we were all related. When I asked my daddy how he was related to someone, he replied, "On my mother's side or on my father's side?" meaning he was kin in more ways than one—like to his cousin John

Graham Webb, who was a Webb; but on their mothers' side, Daddy's and John Graham's grandmothers were sisters. This only confused me more. I resolved the issue by figuring out Daddy's first cousins and just accepting on faith that somehow we were kin to all the others.

My great grandfather and grandmother, Joseph Cheshire Webb and Alice Hill Webb, had four sons: Joseph Cheshire Webb, Jr., Thomas Norfleet Webb, Francis (Frank) Blount Webb, and Edwin Hill Webb. There was also a daughter, Maria, pronounced Ma rí ah.

There is a colorful story about how Maria married William Roulhac and died a few days after giving birth to a son, following a difficult pregnancy. Shortly after her death, her nurse turned up pregnant with Roulhac's child. All the Webb brothers called on Mr. Roulhac and told him he and the nurse had better be on the 7:00 PM train out of town. They were.

Thomas Norfleet was my grandfather, but I never knew him. From my grandfather, we had two possessions that intrigued me. We were all christened in his beautiful christening gown with lots of tucks and lace and embroidery. Daddy also had a journal of his father's expenses when he was at the University of North Carolina. Grandfather lived in a dorm right beside the famous old well at the center of campus, and each week he would take his shirts and collars down to the well, where women from town would pick them up and take them home to launder them. In those days, shirts had removable collars that could be washed and ironed without having to do the whole shirt. My grandfather's weekly laundry list was in the journal. The last page of the little book had the name and address of the girl who was to be my grandmother. We also had his pocket watch that, when I was a child, hung in a little glass dome on a table in the living room.

I never knew my grandmother, Anne Ruffin Peebles Webb, because she also died young, the same year my grandfather died. She also was called by her double name and people referred to her as Annie-Ruffin or Miss Annie-Ruffin or Annie Norfleet, because there were a lot of "Anne Ruffins" in the extended family. Once, I tried to count all the gravestones in the St. Matthew's churchyard that had the double name "Anne Ruffin" before their last name. I gave up.

My grandfather's brothers, our great uncles, died as relatively young men, so we never knew them. However, they had married remarkable women that we were privileged to know: Aunt Eliza (Mrs. Joseph Cheshire Webb, Jr.) of Hillsborough, Aunt Gertrude (Mrs. Frank Webb) who lived in Durham, and Aunt Freda (Mrs. Edwin Webb) who lived in Raleigh. Their children, of course, were my daddy's first cousins—the ones I could keep track of.

My mother was from Florida. Her father died in Jacksonville, Florida, of influenza in the great pandemic when she was a child, so we did not have a grandfather on either side. I always regretted not having a grandfather and was a little bit jealous of my friends who had them.

My mother's mother was my only living grandparent, Florence MacVicar Cooke. My daddy and Uncle Wallace, who was married to my mother's sister, called my grandmother "Miss Flossie." When I was a little girl, (I was born in 1939 and moved to Florida in 1950, so for all these stories I was between 2½ and 11.) my grandmother was a housemother at McIver Hall, a women's dormitory at the University of North Carolina in Chapel Hill. I loved to visit her there, where so much was happening all the time with the students coming and going. In the evenings, I liked to sit in the reception area with the student on duty when the gentlemen would come to call. The boy students would come in and call their dates on the house phone. Then they would wait around until the girls would come down. The college boys would talk to me while they waited, asking me how I liked college life, what I thought about the

Tar Heel football team, what I wanted to be when I grew up and things like that.

My favorite boy was a drama student who dated a girl in my grandmother's dorm. I think he was one of my grandmother's favorites too. When he was in a play, my grandmother would invite me to spend the night and we would go to the theater to see him act. His name was Andy Griffith. He later became a TV star and a favorite son of North Carolina.

There was a low stone wall all around the dorms. I loved to walk on it, to observe campus life and daydream about when I would be a student there. I was allowed to cross the street beside McIver Hall, walk around the campus arboretum and watch the students scurrying to class, or leisurely returning from class licking ice cream cones and drinking Coca-Colas.

The housemothers at Carolina had dinner together at Spencer Hall, a women's dorm that had a dining room. When I was visiting, I dressed up and went to dinner with the housemothers in a little dining room beside the big room where the students were served. I felt very grown up.

The ladies also played bridge together and entertained with tea and cookies, or with sherry or port. Once, when my grandmother had returned from vacation at Black Mountain, she served port wine to the ladies from a beautiful ruby-red, cut-glass decanter with tiny matching glasses that she had bought in the mountains at an antique auction. Grandmother let me have a taste of the port in one of the glasses. It was delicious.

My daddy's two sisters lived in Raleigh. Aunt Gyp—Alice Hill Webb, named for her grandmother—was married to Uncle Doc, Dr. Verne Strudwick Caviness. Aunt Annie's real name was Anne Ruffin Webb, named for her mother; but people called her Annie or Annie Ruffin, or Red or Lade—short for lady. Aunt Annie was not married, but she had lots of boyfriends. When I was a little girl, my mother's sister, Aunt Sally, married Uncle Wallace, Wallace Emory Seeman; they lived in Durham. My aunts, who remained close to Hillsborough and who visited often, played a major role in my life. With them, I had most special relationships. I loved them profoundly. They were excellent role models and gave me advice and counsel as long as they lived. I tried to be like them because I admired their generous spirits, their sense of fairness, their caring, giving and sharing nature. I enjoyed their sense of humor and loved to laugh with them. Even though I always wanted a grandfather, I would not have traded the aunts for a dozen grandfathers!

Family Tree

When my grandparents, Thomas Norfleet Webb and Anne Ruffin Peebles, married, they brought together two old and distinguished North Carolina families—on the one side, the Hoggs/Huskes, Webbs, Cheshires, Hills, Strudwicks etc. On the other side, the Bennehans, Camerons, Kirklands, Ruffins and Peebleses etc.

Sally Ann Webb McPherson

Stagville

Richard Bennehan

Dominick Bennehan (died 1716)
married
Elizabeth Dudley
Elizabeth, Alexander, Frances, Dudley
|
their son
|
Dudley Bennehan (1713-1749)
married **"Rachel"**
Dominick, Alexander, William
Dudley, Richard, Betty, George
|
their son
|
Richard Bennehan (1743-1825)
married in 1776
Mary Armis (1756-1812)
Rebecca, Thomas Dudley
Snow Hill Plantation
Brick House (Mount Union) Plantation
Built Stagville in 1799
|
their daughter
|

Duncan Cameron
married
Margaret Bain
Elizabeth, Alexander, Frances, Dudley
|
their son
|
Reverand John Cameron (1745-1815)
married in 1733
Anne Owen Nash (1753-1825)
Mary Read, Duncan, Jean, Anna, John Adams,
William Ewen, Dr. Thomas Nash, Margaret
|
their son
|

Duncan Cameron, Fairntosh

Rebecca Bennehan (1778-1843) married in 1803 **Duncan Cameron** (1777-1853)
Mary Anne, Thomas Armis Dudley, Paul Carrington, Margaret Bain,
Rebecca B., Jean Syme, Anne Owen, Mildred Coles
Built Fairntosh in 1804, and house in Raleigh in 1838

Paul Carrington Cameron

Anne Ruffin Cameron, Burnside

their son

Anne Ruffin (1814-1898)
married in 1832
Paul Carrington Cameron (1808-1891)
stillborn, stillborn, Jean, Rebecca B., Anne Ruffin, Mary Armis,
Duncan II, Margaret B. Duncan III, Pauline Carrington,
Bennehan, Mildred Coles
Built Burnside, 1830s
|
their daughter
|
Margaret B. Cameron (1848-1896)
married in 1875
Robert Bruce Peebles (1840-1916)
Anne Ruffin Peebles (ne child)
|
their daughter
|

Cameron Sisters - Paul & Anne's daughters

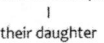
Robert Bruce Peebles

Anne Ruffin Peebles (1876-1928)
married 1901
Thomas Norfleet Webb Sr. (1877-1928)
Robert Peebles, Alice Hill, Rebecca Norfleet,
Thomas Norfleet Jr., Anne Ruffin

12

Warm Firesides Wide Porches

Ayr Mount

William Kirkland (1768-1836)
married in 1792
Margaret Blain Scott (1773-1839)
Anne McNabb, Elizabeth Machen, Margaret Scott,
William, Jane Rebecca, William, John Umstead,
Martha Shepard, James, Alexander McKenzie,
Mary Anderson, Susannah Umstead,
Phebe Bingham, David
Built Ayr Mount in 1815
|
their daughter
|
Anne McNabb Kirkland (1794-1875)
married in 1809
Thomas Carter Ruffin (1887-1870)
Catherine Roane, William Kirkland, Anne, Alice Roane,
Sterling, George McNeil, Peter Browne, Elizabeth,
Thomas Carter, Jr., Susan Mary, Jane Minerva,
Martha Phebe, Dr. John Kirkland, Sally Nash
Hermitage Plantation 1829
|
their daughter

*Thomas Ruffin,
St. Matthews
Episcopal Church*

*Annie Ruffin
Peebles and
Thomas Norfleet
Webb*

Research and layout of the family tree by Margaret McPherson.

Sally Ann Webb McPherson

Isaac Hill I (1636-1710)
married "unknown"
Martha, Michael, Isaac II, John, Nathaniel
|
his son
|
Isaac Hill II (1670-1734)
Married "unknown"
John Hill, Isaac Hill III
|
his son
|
John Hill
married in 1760
Martha Whitmel (1723-1762)
Whitmel, Elizabeth, Henry, Mary,
Winifred, Sarah, [sic] child
|
their son
|
Whitmel John Hill (1743-1797)
married his first cousin around 1760
Winifred Blount (1743-1799)
daughter of Thomas Blount
first cousins, their mothers were sisters
John (died young), Joseph (died young),
Thomas Blount, Martha Elizabeth
|
their son
|
Thomas Blount Hill (1775-1815)
married
Rebecca Norfleet (1783-1845)
Rebecca Norfleet, Marie Louise,
Whitmel John, Marie Antoinette,
Rebecca Whitmel, Eliza Blount,
Thomas Blount, Winifred Blount
|
their son
|
Thomas Blount Hill, Jr. (1813-1888)
married in 1836
Maria T. Simpson (1812-1871)
Elizabeth, Rebecca Norfleet, Sarah Simpson,
Thomas Blount III, Mary Louise,
John Boyd, Mary Alice
|
their daughter
|
Mary Alice (1853-1931)
married in 1877
Joseph Cheshire Webb (1848-1893)
Thomas Norfleet, Joseph Cheshire Jr.,
Whitmel Hill, Francis Blount, Maria Hill
|
their son

Court House

John Gray (1690-1750)
married
Ann Bryan (1698-1770)
|
their son
|
William Gray (1730-1801)
married 1754
Frances Lee
|
their daughter
|
Joseph Blount II (1755-1794)
married 1782
Ann Gray (1754-1814)
|
their daughter
|
John Cheshire II (1769-1830)
married 1812
Elizabeth Ann Blount (1790-1869)
Mary Frances, Joseph Blount, John Cox,
Wilson Godfrey, Eleanor Blount,
Sarah, Frances, Elizabeth,
Anne, John,
Thomas Cox
|
their daughter

James Blount (-1686)
married
Anne Willis (-1700)
|
their son
|
John Blount (1669-1725/6)
married in 1695
Elizabeth Davis
Mary, Elizabeth, Martha Ann,
Ruth, Sarah, Hester,
Anne, John, Rachel, James,
Joseph, Charlesworth, Benjamin
Thomas, Esau, Jacob, Joseph
|
their son
|
Joseph Blount I (1715-1777)
married 1752
Elizabeth Scarboro
|
their son
|
John Cheshire I (1779)
married 1759
Mary Francis Miller
Mary, stillborn,
Margaret, John
|
their son

Bellevue Cotton Mill

Mary Alice
Hill Webb

Hillsborough,

Warm Firesides Wide Porches

Giles Webb
|
his son
|
John Webb married **Mary Sanford**
|
their son
|
James Webb (1673-1716) married **Sara**
|
their son
|
James Webb (1705-1771)
married in 1731
Mary Edmondson of Essex, VA (1712-1795)
James, Mary, William, John, Thomas, Eliabeth
|
their son
|
William Webb (1745-1809)
married in 1771
Frances Young
Rachel, James, William S.,
John, Thomas, Henry, Mary E.,
Henry Young, Frances,
Samuel Smith
|
their son
|
James Webb, M.D. (1774-1855)
married in 1807
Anne Alves Huske (1785-1852)
Henry, Frances, Helen, Elizabeth, Anne, James,
William (died at two), John Huske,
Mary, Dr. William, Thomas
|
their son
|
James Webb (1816-1897)
married in 1842
Sarah Francis Cheshire (1822-1891)
John Cox, James, Elizabeth Cheshire,
Annie Huske, Joseph Cheshire Webb,
Sarah Frances, Helen Long,
Mary, Eleanor Blount, Margaret Taylor,
Caroline Winder, Henry Winder
|
their son

Presbyterian Church

Thomas Ingles
married
Margaret Scott
|
their daughter
|
Alexander Alves (-1734)
married 1724
Elizabeth Ingles
|
their daughter

Dr. & Mrs. James Webb

Gavin Hogg (About 1700-)
married in Scotland
Helen Stevenson (About 1705-)
Robert, John, James
|
their son

James Hogg

James Hogg (1729-1804)
married in 1724, Scotland
Elizabeth McDowell Alves (-1801)
Eizabeth Alves Hogg, Helen Alves
Hogg, Walter Alves, Gavin Alves,
Robina Alves Hogg
|
their daughter
|
Elizabeth Alves Hogg (1725-1788)
married in 1784
John Huske (-1892)
Anne Alves Huske, John Huske II
|
their daughter

Hillsborough ("Aunt Eliza") House

Thomas Norfleet Webb House

North Carolina

Hillsborough

Hillsborough was a small town where everybody knew everybody. Adults knew what child belonged to whom and would not hesitate to comment on behavior or tattletale to parents.

In the 1940s, the United States of America was at war with Germany and Japan. However, if adults mentioned "the war" you had to pay close attention because they might be speaking about the Revolutionary War or the Civil War. Those wars were still a part of their lives and were just as real to them as the current one. That's probably because Hillsborough had so many historical markers all over town to remind them of places and people and actions in history. I think it is also because Southerners are renowned story-tellers, and oral traditions preserved the memories for them.

Men gathered at The Corner Drug Store to discuss business and world events and drink Coca-Colas made with a squirt of syrup and carbonated water, 5 cents.

The Corner Drug Store was aptly named because it sits at the corner of the two main streets of Hillsborough: Churton Street and King Street.

Across Churton Street to the east was Mitchell's Hardware, another gathering place, especially for men. Across King Street to the south was the fabric and sewing store—a favorite with the women. Kitty-cornered from the drug store was the historic Orange County Courthouse. In the tower on top of the courthouse was a famous clock that had been in Hillsborough since before the Revolutionary War. The story goes that it was a royal gift to the town, presented by King George III in about 1767. It was so valued that when there were rumblings of war with England, citizens removed the clock from where it hung in the old St. Matthew's church and buried it in a safe spot until the war was over. When the new courthouse was built in the 1840s, the clock was moved to hang in the cupola there. The boldly handsome clock—with a black face, gold hands and large gold Roman numerals—still marked the hours for everyone downtown in the 1940s.

Courthouse Clock

Our friend Jake Forrest owned The Corner Drug Store. He was a pharmacist. When he was called to war, Jake served in the Navy as a pharmacist there too. While he was away, Miss Sue Hayes, the retired previous owner of the drug store, returned to her role as pharmacist. I was happy when Jake came home safely from the war. Our neighbor and postmaster, Tom Bivins, lost a leg and came home from the war in a wheelchair.

Jake was funny. The men laughed when he told his mother he had to go to a Wildlife Society meeting. She thought he was a member of a group caring for wild animals, when he was really going out partying in Chapel Hill.

I liked to be at The Corner Drug Store when the men took a break from their work and gathered there. They teased me a lot. I was an outgoing, independent, feisty child with red hair and freckles, who obviously enjoyed their company and being teased. Mr. Chance, who owned the Osbunn Theater, had a standing dime bet that I could not whistle and look at him; Jake told me that my widow's peak and cow lick were where the angels kissed me; the men would pat me on my red head, saying it was good luck. They insisted that if I kissed my elbow, I could turn myself into a boy. They laughed as I tried and tried to kiss my elbow, because all my friends were boys.

On Saturday afternoons the men were at the drug store to listen to college football games on the radio and engage in friendly rivalry and an occasional wager. Sometimes I bet the nickel I had brought for popcorn or a Coca-Cola on my favorite team, the University of North Carolina and my favorite player, Charlie "Choo-Choo" Justice, a famous All-American player at the time. Sometimes I won, sometimes I lost. Usually I would rather have popcorn than gamble.

Down the hill from the drug store, beyond the fabric store, was the post office. Townspeople went to the post office to pick up their mail.

We did not have home delivery. You could count on seeing just about everybody at the post office, especially if you went mid-morning after the mail had been put up. Incoming mail awaited pick up in brass boxes that had combination locks and little switch-like handles. Our box was a regular, small box. I knew the combination and how it worked. Sometimes I was permitted to open our box and fetch the mail. Daddy's cousin, Boo Collins, (her real name was Elizabeth) had a much bigger box on the bottom row, because hers was a business box and she received lots of mail. If you needed stamps, or wanted to have a package weighed, or if you had gotten a notice that you received something too large for your box, you went to the window for help. Stamps to mail a letter were three cents; stamps for a post card cost a penny.

Milk was delivered to your back porch in glass bottles. The rich yellow cream rose to the top of the bottle. You had to shake it to mix it with the milk again. Or you could pour the cream off the top for use in sauces or coffee, or to make whipped cream.

Families kept an account at the local grocery store. We would call the grocery store and order our groceries by telephone. Then they would be delivered to our home. When my mother was a young bride, she ordered chicken. It was delivered alive and left on the back porch with its feet tied together. The chicken scared her to death! She did not know what to do with it. After that, if my mother ordered chicken, she was careful to specify a "dressed" chicken.

We could also go to the grocery store with our list, and the grocer would take the items from the shelves for us and put the charges on our account, to be paid at the end of the month. We could take the groceries home if we had only a few items, or the grocery store would deliver them for us.

Three medical doctors had offices in Hillsborough. However, they also made house calls visiting the sick and delivering babies at homes all throughout the countryside. They were the classic country doctors who traveled at all hours of the day and night and in all kinds of weather with their black leather doctors' bags in tow.

Our dentist had an office up steep stairs above The Corner Drug Store.

Telephone numbers were three digits. Miss Mamie Gordon operated the town switchboard. We would ring our phone and Miss Mamie would say, "Operator." Then, we would tell her what number we wanted. Or, we could always call her if we needed to find our mother. She knew everything.

Homes had one telephone, usually in a central location, like in a hallway. Some families were on a "party line," which meant they shared a line with other people, usually neighbors. When we picked up the telephone to use it, others might already be on the line and we could hear their conversation. It was impolite to listen to other people on your party line. We were supposed to hang up and wait for the them to finish their conversation, or their business. My mother was strict about telephone etiquette. However, there was no way to tell if a party were still on the line, so if we were impatient, we naturally picked up the receiver often.

Our small downtown was a busy place on Saturday afternoon. The country people came to town from outlying farms, and mill workers came from West Hillsborough, where the cotton mills were located, to do their shopping, get haircuts and shoe shines, and go to the movies.

Saturday afternoon movies were generally cowboy movies with Roy Rogers, Gene Autry, Hop-a-Long Cassidy, Lash LaRue and the like. I especially liked the Roy Rogers and Gene Autry movies because they sang songs like *Home on the Range, Don't Fence Me In, Streets of Laredo, Tumbling Tumbleweed* and other cowboy songs. At the movie house, first came the newsreels. "News of the World" showed pictures and stories of what had happened in the world that week; that is where we saw pictures from the war, pictures of the war effort on the home front and pictures of world leaders. Next, there was always a serial: a short story that ended at a suspenseful part so moviegoers would wonder what was going to happen and come back next week to see the continued story. Then a cartoon played, followed by the featured movie.

The colored people sat in the balcony and the white people downstairs. Movies cost nine cents and popcorn cost five cents. After the movies, most of the children would come to our big yard, where we would re-enact scenes from the movie.

On Saturday afternoons in the fall, while we were at the cowboy movies, lots of adults went to college football games or listened to them on the radio. Most people in my family were Carolina fans, but some people liked Duke or North Carolina State. My Uncle Wallace, who went to Duke, was a Duke fan and so was Uncle Doc. Uncle Doc had attended Duke University when it was named Trinity College.

Our country was at war in Europe and in the Pacific, far away. Yet the war was a real part of our everyday life. Meats, sugar, coffee, shoes, gasoline and other staples were in short supply because of the war. They were rationed, meaning that we could get only our individual rations, or shares. It worked like this: Families were issued ration stamp books with the allocation of stamps depending on how many people were in the family and what our wartime need for rationed items was. When someone wanted to buy a rationed item, she must give the merchant the corresponding number of ration stamps. Once the stamps were used, we did not get more until the next issue.

We prayed for the soldiers, sailors, Marines and for the President of the United States; we sang patriotic songs. Children all knew the official songs for the Army, Navy, Army Air Force and Marines. Sometimes parents would wake sleepyhead children with the words to Reveille—the bugle call that awoke the soldiers:

You've got to get up
You've got to get up
You've got to get up this morning . . .

Sally Ann Webb McPherson

We collected tin foil from gum wrappers to be used to jam radar signals. We had kin, neighbors and friends fighting in the war, and we tried to follow where they were with maps and a globe. My brothers had a large picture book showing photos of all the Navy fighting vessels.

The flag of the United States of America had 48 stars—six rows with eight stars per row. When we said the Pledge of Allegiance to the flag, it was "and to the Republic for which it stands, one nation, indivisible, with liberty and justice for all." No "under God." "Under God" was added in 1954 and two stars were added in 1959 for the states of Hawaii and Alaska.

Our President of the United States, Franklin Delano Roosevelt, had polio, a crippling disease. I identified greatly with him because I, too, was stuck in a wheelchair or bedridden with a staph infection of the bone. I enthusiastically and persistently collected money for the March of Dimes, to fund research to find a cure for polio. People would donate a dime and I would place it in a slot on a cardboard folder. When I filled up the folder, I turned it in at school. I tried to listen to the President's speeches on the radio. I watched him in the newsreels. I thought he was a great man, but my family did not care much for him. At the time, I did not know why, but I did not let their opinion influence my thoughts or affections for him.

Warm Firesides Wide Porches

Osteomylitis

At about age two-and-a-half, I was diagnosed with the staph infection called osteomylitis in my left leg. My doctor was Dr. Beverly Raney, my cousin Bev Webb's uncle. During the war, osteomylitis was common among battlefield injuries. Dr. Raney was a brilliant man who had studied how osteomylitis was being treated on the battlefields. Field doctors would scrape/clean the bone and pack the wound with sulfa drugs; he determined to treat my osteomylitis the same way. I was the first civilian to receive this procedure; therefore, medical journals documented my case. Without this innovative battlefield treatment, my leg would have been amputated.

   I spent many months in Watts Hospital in Durham or at home with a plaster cast until I was about seven years old. I had numerous surgeries during this time and remember having an out-of body-experience during one surgery, where I was above the scene, looking down at what was going on in the operating room. In a brilliant light, I saw the people in sterile masks and gowns bending over my leg. The operating room was stark and the floor was black and white.

Sally Ann in Plaster Cast

I also received many blood transfusions. Some transfusions were direct, meaning I was connected directly to the person donating the blood and the blood flowed in clear tubes between us. My daddy and his cousin, Ed Strudwick, had type O-Negative blood like me, so they often gave me direct transfusions.

As a result of my illness, I received a lot of special attention. I was outgoing and friendly, with a notably inquisitive and independent nature.

I would be admitted to the hospital again and again. The doctors, the nurses, the technicians—even the maids and janitors—were my friends. They would come by to say hello and check on me even when they did not have to. There were always new student nurses and new medical interns. When I was admitted, unless I was too sick to be in the ward, I always had the same spot—across from the nurses' station by a window overlooking a reservoir, with a smoke stack also in view. Once, a new admitting nurse put me in a different spot, beside the nursing station. From that spot, I could not observe all the activity at the nurses' station; there was no window and no view outside. I borrowed the nurse's scissors and proceeded to cut off one of my pigtails and one of the auburn pigtails of a beautiful Madame Alexander doll named Judy that my aunts had brought me. My mother fixed the doll's pigtail, but my own other pigtail had to be cut.

Another incident involving scissors happened at home when I switched from cutting paper dolls to carving up my bedspread. This rebellious action occurred after I was left too long unattended while confined to bed and weighted there by a thigh-to-toe plaster cast. "I thought that would hurt your feelin's," I reportedly told my mother.

When the osteomylitis was in remission and I had no cast on, I was tough and thought I could do anything my big brother and his friends could do.

Clothes

My mother was a talented seamstress, and I felt lucky that she liked to sew for me. On many dresses, she did smocking, a style of embroidery or decorative stitching that gathered the fabric in sort of a honeycombed pattern across the front. These dresses had wide sashes tied in the back and deep hems that could be let out as I grew. My mother made bloomer-style underpanties to match the dresses—a good thing for a little girl who climbed trees and hung upside down.

I was also fortunate that I had girl cousins three years older than I who were spiffy dressers and who sent me their hand-me-downs. My cousin Betsy in Raleigh sent me clothes and accessories in every hue and shade of blue—it was her favorite color and I don't think she wore other colors. My cousin Patricia in Florida seemed to enjoy a wider palette of colors— I particularly remember one Sunday-go-to-meeting dress made of pale peach-colored embroidered organdy. It was so beautiful that I never wanted to outgrow it.

For everyday shoes, I wore brown oxfords—a sturdy leather shoe with laces on top. For dress up, all little girls wore black-patent leather "Mary

Janes" with white sox. Sometimes we had tennis shoes, or Keds for play, but shoes were rationed because of the war and the oxfords were more versatile.

Shoe stores were equipped with a fluoroscope machine for fitting. We tried on the shoes and then stepped on the machine with our feet under a special light making it possible to see our feet and toes tucked in the shoes. I had wide feet, double Es, and we usually had to go to the mountains or order from a catalog to get shoes to fit me. I thought it was a waste to use our ration stamps on a pair of shoes when I had need of only the right shoe because my left leg was in a cast. Wouldn't it be more practical if I could get two different right shoes instead of a pair?

Young boys wore short pants or knickers. I remember when Skippy got his first long pants. He was so proud and handsome in them. Boys also got to wear overalls, dungarees and T-shirts. They almost always had canvas tennis or basketball shoes as well as oxfords.

In winter when it was cold, or when it snowed, both boys and girls struggled to pull on leggings, which were tight-fitting, heavyweight wool pants that zipped up at the bottom on the legs. Leggings also had a strap that fitted under your foot to hold the pants leg down around your ankles. These britches were not comfortable. Usually, a heavy wool, fitted jacket for girls or double-breasted coat for boys matched the leggings. When that outfit got wet, it smelled awful, much worse than a wet dog! Of course, I could never wear leggings when my leg was in a cast.

Religion

My family was Episcopalian and we attended St. Matthew's Church. St. Matthew's was beautiful. It had warm woods and cathedral ceilings, magnificent stained-glass windows, including one by Tiffany, ornate shiny brass altar rails, red carpet and red velvet prayer kneelers. It made you feel holy and worshipful just to be there.

It seemed to me that not many people besides our extended family attended church at St. Matthew's. The minister's family, my friend Margaret Ray's family, Mrs. Roberts and the country children Miss Annie Cameron brought to church were the only non-family people I knew at St. Mathew's. Miss Annie, my daddy's cousin, drove out into the country on Sunday morning and picked up children who otherwise would not have been able to go to church or Sunday School.

Sunday School was taught on the front and back pews of the church. Miss Annie taught the younger children; the minister's wife, Mrs. Masterton, taught the other class. Mrs. Masterton wore beautiful wide-brimmed hats that looked marvelous on her. She was extremely animated. She loved to teach about Saint Paul—she could channel him to a T, making him and his teachings come alive. It was quite a transformation to see this graceful and elegant southern lady become Saint Paul!

We had colored people who attended our church too. Usually they were older people who had worked for family members for a long time. They sat in the balcony. I always thought the balcony had the best seats.

I liked to sit beside my cousin Beverly Webb at Sunday school. He was my brother's age, but he was nice to me. Bev would always share his hymnbook and point to each word—even before I could read. Margaret Ray, who was my age, would sing *Onward Christian Soldiers* no matter what the hymn was, because she knew all the words to *Onward Christian Soldiers* by heart.

My daddy always gave us ten cents for the collection plate. Paul Cameron asked why. Daddy told him it was for the work of the church and to pay the minister.

Everyone in town knew the story that on one Sunday, right in the middle of prayers, Paul Cameron walked down the aisle right up to the kneeling minister, tugged on his sleeve and said in a loud voice, "Mr. Masterton! Mr. Masterton! Here's your pay." There are other versions of this story, as often happens when stories involve a character like Paul Cameron, and when stories are repeated over and over. One version of this story has the offering amount being five cents. On Sundays, Daddy gave us each a dime for church and a nickel for a treat at the drug store. So, it is entirely possible and plausible that Paul Cameron reversed the amounts.

When you had a birthday, the minister called you to the altar, put his hand on your head and said a special prayer just for you. In January, my brother Paul Cameron, my cousin Katesy Webb, and I—all three—had birthdays—I was the oldest and my birthday was January 29; Katesy was one year younger than I and her birthday was January 28; and Paul

Cameron was a year younger than Katesy and his birthday was the 27th. So, on the last Sunday in January we three went to kneel at the altar; one-by-one, the minister put his hands on our heads and said the birthday prayer. It was a nice enough prayer:

> Watch over thy child, O Lord, as her days increase; bless and guide her wherever she may be, keeping her unspotted from the world. Strengthen her when she stands; comfort her when discouraged or sorrowful; raise her up if she falls; and in her heart may thy peace which passeth understanding abide all the days of her life.

I took issue with the "keeping her unspotted from the world" part. Why? Didn't God want us to strive to be the best, to use our talents to their fullest? How can you be a famous doctor, or teacher or singer, or President of the United States and be unspotted from the world? My parents told me not to worry about it, but I wished they would leave that part out!

Before church, all the men would stand outside talking and smoking until the church bell rang, when they came in and joined their families. Everyone sat in the same place every Sunday—on their pew. Our pew was the next to the last row on the left side in front of Cousin Mary and Cousin Paul. We could always look around and see who was in their spot and who was missing.

St. Matthew's had a beautiful churchyard. There was a red brick wall with a curved top all around it. We had lots and lots of family buried there, but I could not keep all the living relatives straight in my mind, much less the dead ones. My grandparents had a handsome, but plain, gravestone. I secretly liked much better the more ornate, marble stones with carved flowers and birds and angels and poetry. Once, we had our church picnic in the churchyard, but we were not allowed to walk on the graves. That was disrespectful.

Hillsborough had a Presbyterian Church, a Methodist Church, a Baptist Church and a colored church. All the churches had much larger congregations than ours. During the summer the Presbyterians, the Baptists and the Methodists all had Bible School and we children went to them all. I even remember going to Raleigh and attending Methodist Bible School with my cousins, because my Uncle Doc was Methodist. At Bible School, we learned all the Bible stories, memorized obligatory Bible verses and put on programs for our parents. Sonny Williams' mother brought in food that was as close as you could get in rural North Carolina in the 1940s to what the Jewish people ate on their wanderings in the wilderness on their way to the Promised Land. We had crackers instead of unleavened bread, black grapes and a hard cheese that was unfamiliar to most of us children. Maybe Mrs. Williams knew the way to a child's brain is through the stomach.

Episcopalians didn't talk much about hellfire and damnation, but the other churches did. My brother's friend, Bruce Richmond, was a Methodist, and he told me all about hellfire and damnation. He introduced me to the concept of eternity and said that people who did not live right would be damned and they would burn in hellfire forever and forever and forever in eternity. This bothered me—not so much the burning, but the never-ending eternity part. Even if heaven meant floating around on a fluffy white cloud in a Carolina-blue sky, I did not think I wanted to do that for eternity either. Wouldn't you get bored with no end to it? "Eternity" is a mighty big concept for a little girl to understand.

Hillsborough had one Jewish family, Mr. and Mrs. Jack Blieden, who ran the shoe store. Mr. Blieden had an unusual nickname. Since Hillsborough did not have any Greeks, Dr. Roberts insisted that Mr. Blieden had to do double duty and he called him "the Greek."

I do not think we had any Catholics.

My Great Aunt Clara, who lived in Florida, was Catholic. When she would come to visit, Daddy would drive her to Durham on Fridays for confession of her sins and on Sundays to church. We also got to have fish on Fridays when she came because Catholics did not eat meat on Friday.

One year my friend Joan Forrest went away to a Catholic Girls' Boarding School. She told us about Mass. Mass sounded to me a lot like Holy Communion that we had once a month at St. Matthew's, but the Catholic girls had it every single day. She told us about the Rosary and about Hail Marys. Joan taught us to say the Hail Mary. I thought Mary was beautiful and the perfect mother for Jesus, and I was really glad the Catholics paid her so much attention and so much respect. I did not understand the "blessed is the fruit of thy womb, Jesus" part, though. Why didn't we just say, "blessed is her son, Jesus?" Joan did not know the answer.

Transportation

People walked a lot; they walked for the exercise and, of course, because gasoline was rationed. My friend Nell Beard's father, who was tall and skinny, walked from his home on the east side of Churton Street all the way to the Bellevue Cotton Mill in West Hillsborough and back each day.

There were two car dealerships, General Motors and Ford, but there were no new cars because the factories and plants were dedicated to the war effort making trucks, Jeeps, tanks and the like for fighting the war. Almost all automobiles were black with these exceptions: my mother had a little white Ford coupe; Aunt Annie had a sporty green Pontiac and my daddy drove a wooden-sided Ford station wagon. I liked that their cars were different.

We had service stations where we bought gas and got our car serviced. When we needed gas, we drove up to the pump and the attendant approached the driver's window. "Fill 'er up," the driver would say; or the driver might say how many gallons to put in. Drivers had to have enough stamps as well as enough money because gas was rationed. The attendant would raise the hood of the car and check the oil and water; he would check the tire pressure and wash the windshield, too. I guess that is why it was called a "service station."

At the service station, you could buy Coca-Colas from the ice chest out front. Coca-Colas came in six-ounce green glass bottles with the name of the town where it was originally bottled stamped on the bottom. Inside, you could buy packages of Lance's peanut butter crackers, bags of Tom's salted peanuts, candy bars, chewing gum and tobacco products. Some service stations, especially in the country, also carried staples like milk and bread.

Hillsborough had a busy Trailway's Bus Station across Churton Street from the courthouse, beside the post office. We had a train station in West Hillsborough near the cotton mills.

One year, when Skippy had been at summer camp in New Hampshire, I rode the train with my mother to New York City to meet Skip and bring him home. That was a great adventure! We walked between the clanking train cars and had a lovely, elegant dinner in the dining car; we traveled to the observation car and watched the countryside pass outside the window; we slept all night in a Pullman berth. On that trip, my mother taught me to knit.

I wanted to go to summer camp, but all I got to do was go to Bible School. You didn't get to travel on a train to go to Bible School. At camp, Skippy had special reading lessons; he also learned woodworking and leather and bead crafts. He took archery and learned how to shoot a real bow with real arrows. He went rowing and canoeing and overnight camping. He was so lucky!

Until he came home from camp at the end of summer, we did not learn much about Skip's activities even though he was required to write his parents once a week and had to turn in a letter addressed to them in order to be admitted to the mess hall for Sunday dinner. Week after week, my parents received the same letter: "Dear Mama and Daddy—Love, Skippy."

I didn't know anyone who flew in airplanes and we never saw planes flying overhead—any kind of airplane. That's why I thought it odd that we conducted "blackouts" for civil defense. Fearing a nighttime air raid, homes and businesses practiced going dark. That meant you turned off all lights or covered windows with dark "blackout" curtains or blankets.

Aunt Annie's Sporty Green Car

Daddy's Woody

Mother's White Ford Coupe

Agriculture

Small farms dotted the land outside of town. Cotton and tobacco were the cash crops, but farms also produced livestock, fruits and vegetables. "Truck farming" is a term describing these small farms that produce for the local market. I always thought the name derived from the fact that farmers carted the produce to market in pickup trucks. Truck, my mother told me, also meant exchange or barter in old-fashioned English.

Even in town, agriculture was important. People were encouraged to cultivate "Victory Gardens" to provide their own produce. They harvested fruits and vegetables all summer and fall for their family and to share with friends. The women canned the crops for use in winter.

I never understood the use of the word "canned" since cans were not in any way a part of the process. Some country people said, *put up* as in "I put up twelve quarts of tomatoes today." That made more sense to me. Whatever you called it, canning was hard, hot work, and we children knew to stay out of the kitchen on canning days.

Gleaming glass jars with brass-colored lids packed full with colorful tomatoes, corn, beans, peas, beets, peaches, pears and berries sparkled on pantry shelves. Jams and jellies were also preserved when there was enough sugar.

With meat rationed, many families kept chickens for meat and eggs. The occasional cow, pig or goat provided meat, butter and cheese. Our family had a chicken coop with a fenced-in chicken yard down the hill and away from the house. The hens kept our family in eggs and occasionally our yard man would kill a chicken for a roasted chicken dinner. That is when I learned how graphic is the phrase "like a chicken with its head cut off." We even had a hog pen beside the chicken yard and garnered hams, ribs, bacon and other pork cuts when the pig was butchered. We never had a cow.

Business & Industry

The Hillsborough business district made for a pretty self-sufficient little town with grocery stores, pharmacies, fabric and dress stores, men's clothing and dry goods stores, two hardware stores, a flower shop, a funeral parlor, a movie theater, car dealerships and filling stations. There was a beauty parlor where ladies got haircuts, shampoos and sets, and permanent waves to make their hair curly. The chemicals used for processing permanent waves were awfully stinky; people could smell them for about a week, while the perm set, before the woman was allowed to shampoo her hair.

Men patronized the barbershop for weekly haircuts and shoe shines. We had a dairy with a retail outlet that served ice cream. A bank and insurance agency represented financial institutions. Our hotel was the historic Colonial Inn that had hosted many famous people. Its restaurant was popular with local people and drew out-of-towners who came to enjoy the hearty Southern meals and the charming atmosphere of the Inn. The Hickory House Restaurant featured "blue plate specials," inexpensive meals at a fixed price, but *not* served on blue plates.

Hillsborough even had a livery stable, an ice house and the Occoneechee Speedway catering to the burgeoning stock-car racing phenomenon. Law, dental, medical and educational professions were well represented too.

Occoneechee Speedway

> Occoneechee Speedway was one of the first two NASCAR tracks to open and is the only track remaining from the inaugural 1949 season. The site is now heavily forested in forty-year old pines and sycamores. Visible still are the grandstands that once held thousands of enthusiastic fans and the mile-long oval track where such legends as Fireball Roberts, Richard Petty, Ned Jarrett, Louise Smith and Junior Johnson once spent their Sundays competing in the "Strictly Stock" and Grand National series.
>
> This site is one of only three racetracks on the National Register of Historic Places.
>
> From the web site of the Eno River Association at: http://www.enoriver.org/

Bruce's Five & Dime Store stood out as a favorite with children because it carried candy and toys and many other low-priced goods that we could afford if we saved our weekly allowances. I especially liked the cosmetics counter. I once bought freckle remover there. It did not work. I longed for the day I could wear makeup and cover up those freckles! At the cosmetic counter, the Five & Dime sold Tangee Lipstick, a product that I coveted and that was favored by the older girls. Tangee Lipstick was slightly flavored and went on young lips creamy and clear. Then, miraculously, it slowly changed to a tint matching your own exact coloring. When I tried a friend's Tangee Lipstick, my lips gleamed in a shiny, but pale, pale peach color. It looked beautiful. Our Dime Store was not like the Woolworth's or Kresge's stores in Durham that boasted huge candy counters and steamy lunch counters.

My daddy owned the Hillsborough Flower Shop located between The Corner Drug Store and Mr. Blieden's shoe store. That's how I came to spend so much time downtown. On the streets, I sold newspapers, *The News of Orange*. I sold red crepe-paper poppies for the American Legion on Memorial Day. I collected for The March of Dimes. I sometimes picked up the mail, and I visited with the men in the drug store.

Two cotton mills were located in West Hillsborough near the train station and the Eno River. My Webb cousins' father, Jim Webb, was the president of the Eno Mill, and my friend Nell Beard's father was the president of the Bellevue Mill. Lots of children had parents who worked there. The mills ran all day and all night, three shifts. They made materials for the war effort. Sometimes men who worked at the mills were not drafted to fight the war because their work was considered vital on the home front. During this wartime, many women were employed at the mills.

Our neighbors, the Bivinses, manufactured furniture. I never got to visit the factory and I did not know what kind of furniture they made.

Cousin Paul Collins & Skippy

Visiting

When we were children in Hillsborough, North Carolina in the 1940s, Sunday afternoons were for visiting, not football.

Lots of Sundays, our driveway and backyard would be filled with cars. In winter, everyone would sit in the big living room with a fire in the fireplace, conversations everywhere, children playing on the floor and "bourbon and branch-water" most assuredly a part of the scene. In pleasant weather, the visiting shifted to the east side of our wrap-around terrace that was shaded by a huge pecan tree beside the grape arbor and overlooking the front borders of Daddy's flower garden. The children were everywhere except on the porch. Usually visitors toured the vegetable gardens and Daddy would share the bounty from his garden. I once proclaimed, "Daddy grows every single thing there is to eat, except rice and gravy!"

When we went visiting, my favorite places were Cousin Mary and Cousin Paul Collins', Aunt Eliza Webb's and Sam, Rob and Miss Bessie Kirkland's house.

Warm Firesides Wide Porches

Thomas Norfleet Webb Home

Alice Hill Webb built the home for her son, Thomas Norfleet Webb, Sr. between 1906 and 1908. The house was located on the corner of King Street and Hassel Street and had six pillars towering 22 feet on the King Street side. The six-bedroom home had five bathrooms, a large kitchen with butler's pantry, a greenhouse and a wide flagstone terrace across the front that extended on two sides, becoming covered porches.

Thomas Norfleet Webb, Sr. and Thomas Norfleet Webb, Jr. raised their families in this house. After the Thomas Norfleet Webb Jr., family moved from Hillsborough, the house burned down, on February 2, 1956.

Cousin Mary and Cousin Paul's home had a name—*Highlands*. Cousin was pronounced something like "cudin." Boo Collins was their daughter. (Her real name was Elizabeth.) Boo had a pet name for me. She called me "SallyAnnCallahan!" and this made us both giggle every time she said it. Boo had a sister, Mary Strange Collins Williams, who was married and lived in eastern North Carolina. Mary Strange and her family sometimes came on Sundays, too. Boo had served in the war; she was an officer in the Women's Army Corps, the WACs.

Sally Ann Webb McPherson

Highlands—Paul Cameron Collins' Home

On the site that is now Highlands, Mr. James H. Norwood built a two-room building that served as a classical school from 1844 until 1846. Mr. Norwood sold the property to Mr. Andrew Mickle, who added two rooms and the front porch; he used the house as a residence. Mr. Mickle sold the property to E. D. McNair. Paul Carrington Cameron (my great, great, great grandfather) bought the property in the late 1850s and rented it to various people.

On May 4, 1865, General Joseph E. Johnston surrendered 30,000 Confederate soldiers to William Tecumseh Sherman near Durham. On May 5, Union General Robert H. Anderson's brigade was camped at Mr. James Webb's property across the road from the Cameron house. Severe winds made it impossible to handle paperwork outside. Mr. Cameron gave permission to use his house, which was vacant at the time. In the dining room at Highlands, the last of Confederate soldiers to surrender gave their paroles.

In 1877, Paul Cameron remodeled the house and added rooms to comprise the house as it is today. He gave the home to his daughter, Anne Cameron Collins for her lifetime and then to his grandson and namesake, Paul Cameron Collins. Mr. Collins left the home to his daughter, Elizabeth, who bequeathed it to her niece and namesake, Elizabeth Williams Goode, who resides there with her family.

Lots of people always showed up at Cousin Mary and Cousin Paul's; sometimes they filled up two parlors or all the rockers and swings on the porch until some people had to sit on the front steps.

We usually toured Cousin Mary's flower gardens—I thought she and Daddy had the prettiest gardens on the Hillsborough Garden Tour. In the backyard, there was a humongous chestnut tree that forever was my point of reference for Longfellow's "Under the spreading chestnut tree...." Beyond the front yard, the railroad crossed the property. Cousin Paul would check his gold pocketwatch and tell us when a train was coming. We would go down to watch the train rumble past, powered by a mighty steam engine and ending with a "little red caboose." We would wave at the engineer, who would ring the bell and wave at us.

In one of the parlors was a portrait of an ancestor with a slit in the canvas. The portrait was stabbed by a Yankee during the Civil War.

There were always stories. I was fascinated to learn that Cousin Mary had been a great beauty and that Cousin Paul had shot a man in a duel over Cousin Mary when they were courting.

Cousin Mary and Cousin Paul had a wonderful cook named Margaret Faribault. Margaret made the best fried chicken in the whole town. It was pan-fried, crispy and sumptuous. She told me her secret was that she used lots of pepper, but if that were so, everyone could make fried chicken like that. Margaret Faribault also made the best beaten biscuits. Beaten biscuits—more like crackers than biscuits—are small, hard, sort of flat and quite tasty. They are served at parties as hors d'oeuvres. It was a real treat to have one of Margaret's beaten biscuits with a thin slice of country ham tucked inside.

Beaten Biscuits

The secret to making beaten Biscuits is literally to beat them. In the early days, cooks literally whacked the dough with wooden mallets, ax handles or rolling pins. Some cooks say beat and turn the dough 200 times. Some say beat and turn for ½ hour. Margaret Fairibault used a table-sized contraption called a biscuit brake—a large cast iron machine with gears and cranks and rollers that looked like a torture machine of some sort. Modern cookbooks like *The New Joy of Cooking* and *Martha Stewart Living* advise using a food processor.

Boo Collins' Recipe from the St. Matthew's Episcopal Church Cookbook

4 cups of flour

4 level tablespoons lard (Crisco)

½ teaspoon salt

pinch of baking soda (1/4 teaspoon)

½ cup milk

½ cup water

Sift flour, baking powder and salt. Mix in shortening. Combine milk and water and work into flour mixture slowly. Dough should be stiff and worked until pliable and blistered. Roll out on a floured board ¼ inch thick and cut with 1 inch diameter cutter. Prick tops with fork. Bake on cookie sheet @ 400° until bottoms begin to brown. Reduce heat to 350 degrees and bake until a very light brown. Turn off heat and leave in warm oven to dry out. Makes about three dozen biscuits.

Treat yourself to some Smithfield country ham and invite friends for cocktails.

One Sunday after church we went to Cousin Mary and Cousin Paul's for dinner. Cousin Paul said the blessing like this:

Bless us Oh Lord and these Thy gifts we are about to receive from Thy bounty; (If we ever get any!)

And make us ever mindful of the needs of others. Amen.

I thought it was funny. Cousin Mary did not.

Bellevue—Thomas Blount Hill/Joseph Cheshire Webb Home

The house in Hillsborough that was to become Bellevue was originally a two-room structure; built in the 1790s by James Phillips, a Hillsborough tanner.

The property was purchased in 1853 by Thomas Blount Hill Jr, my great great great grandfather) of Hermitage Plantation, Halifax County.

Mary Alice Hill, daughter of Thomas Blount Hill, Jr., married Joseph Cheshire Webb of Hillsborough the grandson of Dr. James Webb. They raised five children at Bellevue: Thomas Norfleet Webb, Joseph Cheshire Webb, Jr., Whitmel H. Webb, Frances Blount Webb, and Maria Hill Webb.

Joseph Cheshire Webb, Jr., married Eliza Drane of Edenton, and raised his family in the home with his mother, Alice Hill Webb.

Bellevue gradually lost its name, as Joseph Cheshire Webb, Jr. was an investor in the opening of the Bellevue Cotton Dye Mills in West Hillsborough, and the name followed the mill.

In 1989, the property was acquired by Beverly R. Webb. Beverly Webb and his wife did extensive remodeling, renovations and repair to Bellevue, transforming it from a residence into the Hillsborough House Inn, a bed and breakfast establishment.

The Webbs sold Hillsborough House Inn in 1998 and it has reverted to a private residence.

When my aunts from Raleigh came on Sundays, we usually visited at Aunt Eliza's. Aunt Eliza's house had a name too, *Bellevue*. After my grandparents died, Gyp, Annie and Daddy lived with their grandmother at Aunt Eliza's when they were not away at boarding school. My Aunt Eliza was exceptionally beautiful and elegant, and so was her daughter, Elizabeth Matheson. Elizabeth was in Daddy's class at the University of North Carolina. Elizabeth's husband Don had a great sense of humor and always had fun stories or comments on the stories of others. He was also handsome. Their daughter, Lil' Elizabeth, carried the tradition of beauty and elegance. As a child, I don't think she ever got dirty, or maybe that recollection exists because I was there mostly on a Sunday.

Aunt Eliza's house had a swimming pool and a brick recreation room in a garden beside the house. The recreation room had once been the kitchen, separate from the house. I was enthralled by that old kitchen; its huge fireplaces covered almost the entire walls on each end of the building.

Once, someone burned a cross on Aunt Eliza's front lawn in the middle of the night. Townspeople speculated that it was the Ku Klux Klan, but it turned out that it was a cousin. The town policeman identified the perpetrator because he had draped the cross with a white sheet. It turned out that the half-burned sheet was clearly marked with an embroidered monogram that led to the cousin.

Sunday visits at the Kirkland's home, called *Ayr Mount*, were always great adventures. In the 1940s, Sam, Rob and Miss Bessie (Elizabeth) Kirkland, who were brothers and sisters, lived there. They were my daddy's cousins. None of them had married—and there were no other Kirklands—so there was no one to carry on the Kirkland name. People referred to them as "the last of the Kirkland line." Miss Bessie and Rob were skinny and frail looking. Sam was big and loud and a lot of fun. He always told tall tales; you did not know whether to believe them, or if he was just teasing. People in town called Sam "Sunshine"; or, when telling colorful stories about him

Warm Firesides Wide Porches

(and there were plenty), it was likely to be "Ol' Sunshine."

Ayr Mount was built by William Kirkland in the early 1800s. Once a great plantation house and elegant home, it was in extreme disrepair, shabby and seemed to be crumbling in upon itself.

In the 1940s, there were porches on the front and back. The front porch was the scene of gatherings for storytelling and visiting in nice weather. The back porch was rather rickety, and you had to go outside onto that porch to go into a small, add-on kitchen. The kitchen had a cabinet called a pie-safe, with a tin front that had holes punched in it. Miss Bessie usually stored inside it leftover biscuits, or pie, or bread, or something good.

Inside, the house itself was still grand, with wide hallways and stairs, large rooms with fine woodworking, high ceilings and beautiful furniture, portraits and mirrors. I remember being intrigued with the harpsichord in the west parlor; most people I knew had never even heard of a harpsichord. I was also fascinated with a piece of furniture that I suppose was the precursor of modern plumbing. It was a handsome wooden piece that looked like a night side-table, but it was hinged on top and opened so that it resembled a toilet seat. There was a door on the front and a chamber underneath the seat in which to place a slop jar, also called a chamber pot.

Beautiful china, silver, crystal and other household items graced tables and stocked cabinets. Once when *Ayr Mount* was open for the Hillsborough Home Tour, Daddy did a flower arrangement of white lilacs in a pedestal piece of white ironware. Sam gave him that vase. Aunt Gyp had a Waterford crystal decanter and a pair of Waterford wassail bowls from *Ayr Mount*. Wassail bowls look like fancy punch bowls with lids. Daddy had the matching Waterford "lemonade pitcher." I think it was called a lemonade pitcher; because it has a lid to prevent summer flies from enjoying the sweet lemonade.

Outside was even more interesting than inside. There were two barns, horses and other animals, a corncrib and haystacks; in the backyard was an outdoor kitchen dating from the 1800s and, in the side yard, a family cemetery complete with an ornate wrought-iron fence and interesting gravestones. The land sloped gently down to the Eno River in back. In front, a broad lawn spread toward the street and a carriageway (driveway) ran down both sides of the lawn. Also, the bushes along the front edge of the driveway had the best blackberry picking in all of Hillsborough!

Add to all that the fact that Ayr Mount was rumored to be haunted, and no wonder it was a favorite place!

Visitors outdid themselves telling stories on the front porch and in the parlors on those Sunday afternoons, but this is my absolute favorite:

How Ayr Mount survived the Civil War: The Yankee general, General William Tecumseh Sherman, and his army were in the area, and North Carolina people knew of General Sherman's reputation in Georgia. The story goes that an old Kirkland, too old to go to war, was living at *Ayr Mount* with a houseful of women relatives seeking refuge there. The old man mounted a large white horse, bareback, and rode out to meet the Yankees *buck naked!* He told the Yankees that the house over there was an asylum and was filled with crazy people. The Yankees passed it by.

Ayr Mount in the 1940s

Ayr Mount Restored

Ayr Mount was built by William Kirkland, (my great great, great grandfather in 1815 just outside Hillsborough on St. Mary's Road. It is a Federal-style plantation house built of brick, unusual for that era. The house features a two-story central portion flanked by single wings on either side. It has large rooms, high ceilings, a wide staircase and elaborate woodwork. When constructed, Ayr Mount was considered the finest home in central Carolina.

In the 1940s, the house was in considerable disrepair and was inhabited by the last Kirklands to live there: Sam, Rob and Miss Bessie (Elizabeth). At that time, there was a wide porch across the front two-story center of the house—great for visiting and storytelling.

Ayr Mount has been restored to its original grandeur, and the house and grounds are operated under the auspices of the Classical American Homes Preservation Trust.

The Waterford crystal wassail bowls that had belonged to the Kirkland family have returned to Ayr Mount and can be seen on tours there. My Aunt Gyp (Alice Webb Caviness) and Cousin Betsy, (Elizabeth Kirkland Caviness) had given them to the Museum of North Carolina History. Ayr Mount is open to the public. http://www.classicalamerican.org/html/ayrmount.

… Sally Ann Webb McPherson

Vacations

Summer was fun from the day school let out until the day school began again! We played and explored. We took swimming lessons at the University of North Carolina. We went to the public library and read lots and lots. My mother read to us, too. The library, in those days without air conditioning, was always cool. I think that was because it was built of stone and had thick walls. It had painted concrete floors that were sooooo cool. I'd take my shoes off and walk on those cool floors.

Probably the best part of summer vacation was going to the beach! We went for a week or two almost every summer. We would go to Cherry Grove-Ocean Drive, South Carolina. I do not know why we went to South Carolina when North Carolina also had great beaches; I think it was because my mother thought it was safer for children. I loved Ocean Drive. It had wide, hard-packed beaches that cars could drive on. The sand, the water vistas and rolling surf, the starry, starry sky—the beach was magic!

At the beach, we learned about tides and about tidal pools holding fish, shellfish, crabs and other marine life, stuck there until the tide rose to free them. We learned about sloughs that developed in low areas to drain water from tidal pools to the ocean. We learned about undertows and what to do if caught in one.

We walked on the beach and collected shells while watching and naming the shore birds. We rode the waves on heavy canvas rafts. We sailed kites. We built and decorated sand castles. We rode horses and ponies on the beach.

Daddy and the boys fished in the surf. They caught flounder, a flat fish that is sand colored and stays on the bottom, where it looks just like the sand. Flounder start out like other fish—with an eye on each side of its body—then it changes and one eye moves so that, when mature, the flounder is flat and has both eyes on the top of its body.

They also caught whiting, a skinny, silver-colored, boney fish.

One year, sitting on the front porch of our cottage, shelling field peas, I stuck a pea in my nose. I could not get it out! In fact, I probably pushed it further in. All of the adults took a turn at trying to get the pea out. They showed me how to cover one side of my nose, pressing it closed with my finger while blowing really hard through the pea-jammed side. That did not dislodge the pea. At last, my parents took me to a local doctor's office, where the doctor removed the pea with surgical instruments. He gave me a lecture about sticking "foreign objects" in my nose. He explained that when a pea, which is a seed, gets lodged in my nose, it picks up moisture and swells. Soon, it begins to grow, sending out tendrils or branches. The tendrils can grow into my sinuses, causing pain. The bigger the pea plant gets the more dangerous and more painful it is. My sinuses, he said, are close to my brain and that could be very serious!

I never again in my entire life, ever put a "foreign object" in my nose!

PEAS

Southerners have all kinds of peas. We have English green peas; we have field peas, black-eyed peas, conch peas, Crowder peas, cowpeas, purple hull peas, pigeon peas and white-acre peas, to name a few. Sweet peas are not edible. Sweet peas are a pretty flowering plant with pastel-colored flowers and no edible parts.

At the beach, we kept on the porch or on the steps for the walk down to the beach a pair of old, raggedy tennis shoes with no laces. The driveway and the road were not paved. Instead, they were made of broken up shells, sharp enough to hurt your feet. Leaving the shell roads, we walked a pathway through sea oats, vines and other vegetation before we got to the beach.

I observed that beach sandspurs are the largest, toughest and meanest sandspurs ever! They can really put a hurt on someone without shoes! *"Thornballs! Thornballs,"* hollered a friend when attacked by the monsters, thus creating a new and more descriptive moniker for the beasts.

One summer cottage was built on stilts with a carport below. This house stood on a shell road at a low spot. When afternoon showers came through, the road became flooded and impassable. We waded through the flooded area, but cars were forever stalling out in the deep puddle. My Uncle Wallace and Skippy would wade out and rescue the cars. They would look under the hood, dry some wires and hot-wire the car to start again. Skippy thought this was great fun. One day, a bakery truck stalled out and Uncle Wallace and Skippy came to the rescue. The grateful driver gave them a box of fresh bakery doughnuts!

My mother introduced us to an unusual treat at the beach. She gave each of us children a lemon and a fat peppermint stick. She cut a hole in the top of the lemon and inserted the peppermint stick. We squeezed the lemon and sucked the juice up through the peppermint stick, like it was a straw. Oh my! What a treat! It was much better than lemonade. By the time we had sucked all the juice from the lemon, the big peppermint stick was crumbling and we ate it.

Coquinas, or donax, were plentiful on the beach. They were so pretty in their multi-colored pastel shells. When a wave came in, the coquinas would appear at the edge of the shore; when the wave went out, the coquinas would quickly dig into the sand and bury themselves. We would dig up the living shells and put them in a colander from the kitchen. We would harvest a bunch of them and take them to the cottage. Mother would make a delicious cream soup from them, and we would save the shells. When the shells opened, they looked like butterflies. The colors were magnificent.

Something we always did at the beach was to go crabbing. We would drive out to a backwater area or a place where little rivulets emptied into the estuary. There we would catch a mess of blue crabs.

To catch crabs, you securely tie a chicken neck with a long string and drop it into waters known to have crabs. When we feel picking and pulling on the line, we slowly, slowly, slowly pull the line up until we can slip a long-handled crab net under the crab and the chicken neck; and then, we have caught ourselves a crab! Crabbing is much more fun than fishing—more action.

To cook crabs, the cook drops them alive into a pot of boiling water. That instantly kills them. We remember vividly the time my mother did not boil the water before dropping the crabs into the pot. She put the crabs into a large pot filled with tap water, put the lid on and turned on the heat. As the water got hot, the crabs climbed on top of each other, knocked the lid off the pot and climbed out! Pretty soon, crabs were scampering and crawling everywhere—all over the kitchen and dining area—with a few escaping under furniture in the living room. We children squealed, screamed and laughed, trying to catch them.

This became one of our great childhood stories. My mother never could live it down.

Back at home we had so much to do....

Sally Ann Webb McPherson

Tree Climbing

Tree climbing was a favorite pastime and our yard had the absolute best trees to climb! Our magnolia tree was everyone's favorite. It was huge and dome-shaped, with strong limbs drooping all the way to the ground. When we broke through those green boughs and entered the canopy of the tree, we would always find a thick covering of brown fallen leaves and a dusky, earthy smell. The low limbs gave easy access to the wondrous jungle-gym that was the magnolia tree. The limbs under the glossy leafed canopy were bare and smooth with lots of forks to hang upside down on; it also had loose, trailing limbs to swing on. We children knew that tree "by heart" and could fly all over it like monkeys! We played tag in the tree, invented daring acrobatic tricks and carried on important conversations there. Sometimes, when the older children were in school, I would climb to the very tiptop and just sit there and think.

Magnolias, of course, are evergreen trees with those shiny broad leaves providing Christmas greenery in everyone's homes. In summer, magnolia flowers are, at once, large and showy and delicate and fragile. The elegant, translucent, creamy-white flower petals are crowned with golden yellow pollen that shatters and spills from the core after the flower opens fully.

Magnolias smell divinely fragrant with a mild scent reminiscent of lemon. They are my favorite flower!

As children, we had use for the plentiful magnolia seed pods that form and then fall after the flowers die. We would gather arsenals of these pods, which we thought looked just like the hand grenades we saw in war movies and newsreels. We would practice throwing them at targets. Then, when pretending war, we would pull an imaginary cap off the magnolia grenade and hurl it at the enemy target. We also used them as dynamite when reenacting cowboy movies and we wanted to blow up a wagon or a mountainside.

When mature, the magnolia pod bears shiny, bright-red, waxy seeds. I would thread the seeds like beads. Paul Cameron pretended to concoct "poison tea" from these seeds, but I do not know who or what he pretended to poison or if anyone ever tasted it.

Our yard had a southern linden tree that was also a good climber. It was gigantic. Its limbs hung down a steep bank at the edge of our yard, almost to the sidewalk below. Its branches were also smooth, but the first branches were pretty high, so I always had to get a boost up to the lowest limb.

In our side yard, we had a sand pile where we built cities, enacted war scenes, and sculpted cars, castles and animals. A large maple tree shaded the sand pile. Once, with a new delivery of sand piled high, the neighborhood boys were competing to be "great champions" by climbing the maple tree and inching out a limb over the sand pile. To be a great champion, they must jump about eight feet onto the sand pile. I, of course, wanted to be a great champion despite the fact that my left leg was in a heavy plaster cast. The boys gave me a boost up to the lowest limb, and I began pulling myself up to the limb overhanging the sand pile. Fortunately, someone with a grain of sense ran inside and told my daddy, who came running out and forbade me to jump. He got a step ladder and fetched me down. All the time, I cried that I was a great champion and I wanted to jump.

Sally Ann Webb McPherson

Pets

We always had at least one dog. When I was a baby, the family pet was a Chihuahua named Jigger. I never knew Jigger, but there was a story that a painter was working upstairs at our house and Jigger bit him in the seat of his overalls and would not let go. The painter went all the way downstairs with the ferocious little dog clamped on his rear.

The first dog I can remember was Lincoln. Lincoln was a big ol' floppy-doodle, silly Irish setter with dog hair the color of my hair: a copper-gold color. Lincoln would sometimes fetch a stick or a ball, but mostly he just loped around and got hugged and petted.

We had a beautiful, muscular, shiny-black Cocker Spaniel named Joe. Joe was really Skippy's dog. He loved that little boy and followed him everywhere he went. When my mother was looking for Skip, she would call around town to learn if anyone had seen Joe. If Joe was hanging around outside, Skippy was inside. Joe was really well-behaved, and he could do tricks, too—for Skippy.

We had another Cocker Spaniel named Golden Beauty. Beauty was really my mother's dog. Beauty was a good mother-dog, who had a couple of litters of adorable Cocker Spaniel puppies. We did not get to keep the puppies because we already had two dogs. We gave one to the owner of the puppies' father, and my mother sold or gave away the others.

We had a goat, named Billy Goat—always the double name was used. Billy Goat ate all the time. He would also pull a wagon, and we loved to ride in the wagon behind him.

I had a rabbit named Pinky. She was fluffy white but had a pink tint around her eyes. Pinky lived in a pen out by the apple tree. Her pen was wire and had a little wooden hutch at the back where she could go to get out of the weather or to sleep. Pinky was my responsibility, so I fed her, gave her water and kept her cage clean. She liked to be petted. Once when I had her out of the cage playing with her, I put her back in the cage and let go of the spring-hinged door too soon. Slam! The door banged closed and cut off Pinky's little white cottontail. Pinky made a great noise and hopped all the way to the back of the cage in one hop! It didn't even bleed. I felt so bad and went running to the house to tell my mother. We put an antiseptic where the tail had been and my mother said Pinky would be fine. She said our dogs had their tails bobbed on purpose and they survived just fine. Pinky survived this just fine too.

Smokey Joe was a pony given to my younger brother, Paul Cameron, by Sam Kirkland. Sam himself was eccentric, like Paul Cameron. Throughout the South, Sam had quite a reputation as the iconic traveling salesman, ladies' man and whisky drinker. My girl cousins tell tales of Sam's groping, or attempted groping. The Presbyterians would not let their choir carol at his home.

Nevertheless, I liked him. Sam was a great storyteller; he was funny and smart and different from most people. He loved my little brother, probably feeling a kinship with little "Hard Rock." Paul Cameron wanted a pony and Sam gave him Smokey Joe.

Smokey Joe was forever getting out of his fence and running all over

Hillsborough with skinny little Paul Cameron chasing after him. Lots of people have stories about Paul Cameron and Smokey Joe, but this is my favorite:

Once, Paul Cameron ran away on Smokey Joe. Finally, at last Daddy found him—down by the Eno River near the bridge, with a colored boy about his age. The boys had taken a chicken from the chicken coop for their adventure. They knew how to kill the chicken and how to dunk it in boiling water to remove the feathers because they had witnessed that many times. They had somehow missed the step about gutting the chicken before cooking. There they were with their faithful mount, Smokey Joe, roasting the chicken, guts intact, on an open fire beside the Eno River.

Paul Cameron on Smokey Joe

Uncle Who's-It, Uncle Bennehan and Governor Burke

Our house had big rooms, high ceilings, several chimneys and a wide stairway. It made many spooky noises like creaking stairs and floors, clanking pipes, noisy radiators and, sometimes, rattling or howling windows. We affectionately referred to all these sounds as the antics of "Uncle Who's-It," our resident make-believe ghost who I imagined had a long white beard and bushy white eyebrows and who wore a sheet. He was not a scary ghost; he simply made noises so we knew he was there.

There were two pieces of furniture in our house that had names. We never questioned why and I always thought of them sort of like "Uncle Who's-It." There was an unusual walnut chair in our downstairs hall by the telephone; it had a square leather seat but a round back and armrests. The chair was named "Governor Burke." In the big living room, along one wall, was a handsome sofa named "Uncle Bennehan." When I was a child, it never occurred to me that there had been real people named Governor Burke and Uncle Bennehan and that the furniture had been theirs. I just thought those pieces had names like Uncle "Who's-It!"

Uncle Bennehan, The Man

Bennehan Cameron, the man, was the son of Paul Carrington Cameron and Anne Ruffin Cameron and the brother of my father's grandmother, Margaret Cameron Peebles, making him "Great Uncle Bennehan."

Bennehan Cameron was a planter, a lawyer, a railroad and highway builder, an industrialist, a military man and a philanthropist. He was a sportsman who especially liked horse breeding and horse racing.

Uncle Bennehan, the Sofa

Governor Thomas Burke, The Man

Thomas Burke (1747-1783) was a physician, lawyer and statesman who moved to Hillsborough in 1774 from Virginia. He was an early supporter of the American Revolution and was chosen as a delegate to the Continental Congress in 1776. In 1781, he became the third governor of North Carolina. He was captured by the British and imprisoned on James Island near Charleston, South Carolina.

John Huske, the grandson of James Hogg and a Webb ancestor, was an assistant to the governor. He was kidnapped and imprisoned with him in 1781. Huske later became Clerk of the Court for Wilmington and represented the city at the Fayetteville Convention of 1789, which adopted the Federal Constitution.

Governor Burke, the chair, was a gift to John Huske. The Webb family gave the chair to the Hillsborough Historical Museum.

Bugs & Such

Playing in the great outdoors, seeking adventures and being curious led to what children today might think some rather odd pastimes.

Doodle Bugs

On a hot summer day, we would find a doodlebug hole on the red clay bank down by the road. Then we'd pick a wild onion leaf and spit on the end. We'd stick the leaf in the hole and wait. Soon, the leaf would begin to wiggle. That meant the doodlebug had begun chewing on the onion. We would let it chew while we said the required "Doodlebug, doodlebug where have you gone? Your house is on fire and your children are gone." Then, we'd quickly pull the wild onion leaf out of the hole with the doodlebug still chewing. Sometimes, the boys would use them for fishing bait.

Lightning Bugs

Lightning bugs are sometimes called fireflies, but they are really little beetles, not flies. They are colored sort of brown-black with yellow and orange. They do not bite or sting; they just fly around in the warm nighttime air and put on a splendid sparkling show with their blinking taillights.

On summer evenings, after supper and before bedtime, nothing was more fun than catching lightning bugs. We children, equipped with a mayonnaise jar or a jelly jar would run all over the yard chasing lightning bugs and putting them in the jar, with holes punched in the top. Sometimes the boys would pinch the light off their tails and place them on their foreheads, where they continued to glow. Mostly, though, we would take the jar to our bedrooms and watch them blink and glow until we fell asleep.

June Bugs

June bugs are also really beetles with hard, iridescent, shiny green bodies and wings.

June bugs don't bite or sting either. We would look for them in springtime. The best place to find them in our yard was in or around the linden tree. After we caught one, we would turn it upside down and tie sewing thread to one of its back legs then let out about a yard of thread and tie it to one of our own fingers. When the June bug righted itself, it would take off flying. It would fly around and around on its string, to our great amusement.

Lady Bugs

Everyone knows lady bugs are lucky and to find them in your garden is a good sign.

Roly Poly Bugs

We would play with Roly Poly bugs whenever we'd find them. Some people call them Pill Bugs, but Daddy said they aren't insects at all, but are related to crabs and lobsters and other things with hard shells. Roly Polies ball themselves up in a tight ball if you pick them up.

Granddaddy Long Legs

The best place to find Granddaddy Long Legs was on the brick wall at St. Matthew's Church. Before or after Sunday School, we would hunt for them. Granddaddy Long Legs are not scary and they do not bite. They have eight legs, but technically, they are not spiders. They are delicate and graceful like a dancer, and when we'd let them walk up our arms, they'd tickle.

Crawfish, Tadpoles, Pollywogs and Frogs

There was a branch at the bottom of our hill that flowed to the Eno River. I never had "branch" defined for me, but I think of a branch as a stream that is smaller than a creek. Our branch wasn't big and it didn't have a name, but it provided lots of adventures. After navigating around stinging nettle, we would wade in it and jump from rock to rock and make mud slides down the banks into the shallow water. We would lift up rocks and find crawfish underneath. We'd catch frogs and tadpoles. Sometimes we would take tadpoles home and keep them in a jar and watch them morph into pollywogs and eventually into frogs.

Caterpillars, Cocoons and Butterflies

Butterflies played and flittered in Daddy's gardens all the time—all different colors and patterns and sizes. However, the best place to find caterpillars and their cocoons was not in the garden.

Buck Roberts had a mulberry tree in his back yard, not the best for climbing, but if you did climb it, at certain times of the year you could find many caterpillars and many cocoons. As everyone knows, caterpillars spin themselves into cocoons and after a while, butterflies emerge. This process is called metamorphosis, meaning that it changes its physical characteristics, like when a frog morphs from a tadpole to a polywog to a frog. We were never there to see the butterflies come out, but we knew they did. It did not occur to us that we could have cut the twig with the cocoon off the tree and taken it home for observation without harming it so we could be there when the butterfly emerged.

Snakes & Lizards

Boys, including my brother Skippy, like snakes. Once downtown, Skippy pulled a snake from his pants pocket and showed it to another boy, who was so startled he jumped through a plate glass window. Fortunately, no one was hurt, but Skip learned not to share his snakes with anybody without first warning them—even if it was a little grass snake. I did not like snakes, but I was not afraid of them.

Once we went to a circus, and my brothers came home with lizards called chameleons. Chameleons are masters of disguise. They can change colors—brown on brown surfaces, green on a green leaf. They looked like miniature dinosaurs—I think that is why boys like them. All boys like dinosaurs. I didn't care for them so of course my brothers chased me with them, holding them by their tails. All of a sudden, the tails broke off and the lizards almost escaped. My mother is from Florida and she knew about chameleons. She explained that losing their tails is an escape mechanism and that the chameleon would grow a new tail. However, my brothers' chameleons met unfortunate ends before they could grow their tails back. The boys put their boxes too close to the radiator and cooked them.

Snails & Slugs

Believe it or not, we even found fun in watching snails and slugs creep across a shady sidewalk, leaving a trail of slime. What was that slime and why was it there?

Sally Ann Webb McPherson

Maynard's Wagon

Maynard Whitted was a colored man who lived down by the river in a neat house with flowers all over the front porch. Maynard had a mule, a wagon and all the farming implements like plows, disks, rakes, etc. He earned a living farming and by hiring out to prepare the land and plant gardens for other people. He came to our house in the springtime and helped Daddy lay out the vegetable gardens and prepare the ground. He also would come in the fall to butcher a hog.

Whenever the town children would hear the rumbling of Maynard's wagon, we would stop whatever we were doing, run to it and hitch a ride. Maynard was good-natured and treated us to the fun of a wagon ride!

Maynard was also the preacher at the colored church. Once, I was privileged to attend that church. There was a special service that my high school babysitter did not want to miss. She asked permission to take me with her and I went. I loved it! I thought the church was beautiful—as pretty as any of the white churches, except St. Matthew's. The walls and the wooden pews had been polished and polished and polished until they literally glowed. The music was soulful and inspiring.

And then there was Maynard—handsome and impressive in a black suit, white shirt and dark tie; he was very much in charge and respected. After that, whenever I saw Maynard in baggy overalls, driving the mule-drawn wagon, working in the dirt or butchering a hog, I remembered the community and spiritual leader—the handsome, well-groomed man in the black suit.

Maynard and the Children Playing on Maynard's Wagon

Toys

We had the usual toys. We had blocks, Lincoln logs, erector sets and tinker toys to build things. We had bicycles, roller skates, scooters, coasters and snow sleds. We had spinning tops, kaleidoscopes, yo-yos and whistles; we had marbles, jacks and Pick-Up-Sticks. The boys had cars and trucks and toy soldiers and sailors with Jeeps and tanks and ships.

I had dolls. Lots of people gave me dolls when I was in the hospital. I almost never played with them unless we needed children in our reenactment of cowboy movies. There was a mystery, however, associated with dolls left by Santa Claus. Almost always, Mrs. Claus had made a wardrobe of clothes for the doll to match dresses my mother had made for me! I thought Mrs. Claus was pretty clever to do that.

My friends Joan and Ellen Claire played with dolls and paper dolls—I did not see much fun in that when Joan had a perfectly wonderful pear tree to climb.

When I was learning to ride my bicycle, I could not take it out of the yard until I had mastered it on all terrains in our yard. It was hard to ride on grass and gravel and soft dirt. When I finally was permitted to ride on the sidewalk, I was amazed at how easy it was.

Roller skates in those days were a platform with a place for the heel and clamps that fitted the front of the shoe. The platform, of course was on rollers, or wheels. We could adjust the length of the skate and make it fit the front of the shoe by tightening the clamps with a "skate key" worn on a string around the skater's neck.

Hillsborough is hilly and you have to do a lot of tacking, side-to-side maneuvers to keep from going too fast. A favorite place to skate was the courthouse square downtown because it was level in front. We would skate out front and then skate right inside the open door of the courthouse. There was a long corridor, front door to back door. The water fountains were on either side of the front door—one marked "white," one marked "colored." I would skate right over to the one marked "colored" expecting the water to arc from the fountain colored like a rainbow. It didn't.

We also had unusual toys. Paul Cameron had a Flaxi—this is like a snow sled, but it has wheels and you don't need snow to ride on it. Once my mother went to New York City and brought us jumping shoes and stilts. The jumping shoes were sort of like skates but instead of wheels under the platform, there were large springs. They fastened onto your shoe by two straps. You could really bounce in them! The stilts were fun too. Soon, all the children had made their own in all sizes and heights.

Sally Ann Webb McPherson

Sports & Games

We played things like Jump Rope, Jump Plank and Hop Scotch that required almost no equipment—just things you had around. We played Tick-Tack-Toe and Battleship that required only paper and pencil.

At birthday parties, we played Pin the Tail on the Donkey and circle games like Farmer in the Dell and Ring around the Rosie.

We played all kinds of sports and games, but nothing was organized or had a coach. Anytime we had a group of friends and wanted to play a team game we picked two captains and the captains chose their teams. Captains were likely picked by an exercise of elimination where we tapped on fists and recited the ritual, "One potato, two potato, three potato four...." When teams were picked, we didn't want to be the last person chosen, but sometimes we were. The teams were always different and we played with and against all our friends at different times.

We played softball, football and basketball. I got chosen last in basketball. By the third grade, I had stopped playing football—I got stepped on by a boy wearing cleats and it hurt. Anyway, I was the only girl. We played Simon Says, Red Rover and Dodge-Ball. If we played

Croquet, sometimes the adults would play with us.

We played Tag, Dog-On-Wood and Hide and Seek—all these involved someone being "it" and trying to get others "out."

When you play Hide and Seek, the person who is "It" leans against a tree that is home base, eyes closed, and counts to a designated number. We would take turns counting by ones, counting by fives, counting by tens. Then, "It" would call out: "Coming, Ready or Not" and go searching for people. When "It" finds someone, he has to beat that person to home base to get them "out." When he gets someone "out," he shouts: "Ally, Ally In-Free!" to call everyone in to base for another round.

Once when we were playing Hide and Seek, I hid in bushes down behind the chicken house with an older boy who was visiting. He wanted to show me his penis. I had brothers. I had seen penises. That is what makes a boy a boy. I wasn't really that interested. But when he showed me his penis I was truly surprised! It was standing up straight and tall like a wooden soldier. I had never seen anything like it. My brothers' penises were not like that at all. Amazing! As I was about to become exceedingly interested, "It" called out: "Ally, Ally In-Free!" and we returned to the game.

When it was raining or cold, we played inside. We would play board games like Parcheesi, Monopoly, Checkers, Chinese Checkers and Bingo, and card games like Old Maid, Go-Fish, Poker and Canasta.

Sally Ann Webb McPherson

Swimming Lessons at the University of North Carolina

Our parents would not let us swim in the Eno River. It was often red-clay muddy and did not look that inviting. Besides, it had a current. We were not even supposed to go near the river. However, sometimes in the spring, I would follow our branch down to the river and marvel at the tender, soft green moss growing there. Beautiful purple violets with broad dark green leaves bloomed there. I would pick a large, fragrant bouquet.

The Eno River

The Eno River courses 40 miles through Orange, Durham and Wake Counties, dropping 250 vertical feet. It flows ten miles south and then hits the Occoneechee Mountain, where it turns east at Hillsborough. It then flows thirty miles east to Raleigh, where it merges with the Little and Flat Rivers to form the headwaters of the Neuse River. It averages fifty feet wide. The Eno supports an exceptionally high biodiversity, including sixty-one species of fish. For more information visit the web site of The Eno River Association at http://www.enoriver.org/eno/River/index.html.

Since we did not have a community pool in Hillsborough, some of the mothers got together and took turns driving us to Chapel Hill to the University of North Carolina for swimming lessons. We crammed like sardines into every inch of the cars.

Carolina had a great swimming complex with indoor and outdoor pools used to train military personnel, but in summer, the university would teach swimming lessons to children.

First we mastered survival swimming—doing the dog paddle well enough to get across the pool, rolling over and floating on our backs so we could breathe, and holding our breath while we sank to the bottom only to push really hard and bounce back to the top to catch a breath. Then we were ready to progress through Beginners, Intermediate and Advanced classes.

We learned water safety as well as swimming. Never dive or jump in water where you cannot see the bottom or don't know how deep it is. "Buddy Up!" Always swim with a buddy and check on one another. Never jump in to save someone without lifeguard training; instead, wherever you swim, be sure you have lifesaving floats, poles or rope to throw a person in trouble. Protect yourself from sunburn when you swim.

The instructors at Carolina were really good swimmers and even better teachers. First, the instructors would get into the pool while the students would stand on deck and watch a precise demonstration of what they wanted us to do. Then the instructor would stand on deck with us, and we would practice the arm movements and breathing there. When we got into the water, we would hold onto the side of the pool and practice the kicks while the instructor came around and coached us. Then we would stand in the water and practice the arm strokes and breathing. The instructor would demonstrate the swimming style again. Now, this is interesting. Before we got into the pool to try to do it like the instructor, we closed our eyes and imagined seeing ourselves swimming perfectly all the way across the pool.

This was called *visualizing;* it was the way they taught the military people who could not swim. It was sort of like your mind telling your body exactly what to do. We did this for all the different styles of swimming and then for diving. It worked for swimming. But no matter how much I visualized taking three steps to approach the end of the diving board, bouncing off into the air, turning vertical upside down and slicing into the water like a knife with my legs perfectly straight, toes pointed and no splash…when I did it, I made a splash.

We learned the crawl, which is regular swimming that most people do. It involves the flutter kick and an over arm stroke synchronized with turning your head and breathing at the point your arm is coming out of the water behind you.

We learned the breaststroke that utilizes a frog kick and an arm stroke similar to the frog kick, where your arms stay in the water. The stroke is synchronized with breathing when your arms thrust back to your sides.

We learned two styles of backstroke—one like an upside-down breaststroke and one sort of like an upside-down crawl where we'd employ the flutter kick and our arms would rotate like a windmill. Breathing is always easier on your back.

We learned the sidestroke, a restful style of swimming. I could swim this stroke all day. You are on your side and use a scissor kick and an arm stroke that pushes the water easily as you glide forward. This style of swimming is important in life saving because a swimmer can carry another person by using this stroke.

The most difficult style of swimming we learned was the butterfly stroke. It was swum front down—like the crawl and breaststroke—and required learning a new kick called the dolphin kick. It was strenuous, with both arms rotating overhead and entering the water at the same time and that dolphin kick going all the time. I never did swim this for fun because it was just too much work.

Swimming lessons were exhausting. The mothers would pick up worn-out children after lessons, and they would bring us a snack for the drive home. My mother often brought fresh, warm doughnuts. Boy did they hit the spot!

… Warm Firesides Wide Porches …

Reading Aloud

I wish every mother and every teacher could read aloud like my mother. I wish I could read aloud like my mother. She was the best! She read aloud to us children all the time.

Of course she started with Mother Goose Nursery Rhymes—we had a large book with illustrations. She would read us the rhyme and show us the picture, and later, she would show us the words as she read them and we would "read" along with her because we knew the rhymes by heart. When my mother read, we did not need pictures. Everything came alive in our minds without pictures.

Winnie the Pooh, Wind in the Willows, Little Black Sambo were early stories. I loved *Winnie the Pooh!* He may have been a bear of very little brain, but he was a good friend and he did have great adventures. I truly never had a passion for *The Wind in the Willows*—it was just too pastel. *Little Black Sambo* would not be politically correct in the modern day, but there were lessons learned there about Sambo's pride in his fine clothes and the tigers' fighting over who was the grandest tiger in the jungle. I liked the purple umbrella and the repetition of "Now I am the grandest

Sally Ann Webb McPherson

Tiger in the jungle!"

My little brother's favorite story was *Pigs is Pigs* about guinea pigs that were shipped as pets and the baggage clerk who wanted to charge the farmer for real livestock pigs. Both the baggage clerk and the farmer were stubborn and ornery. The guinea pigs remained at the train station and multiplied! They kept having babies until they were everywhere! And the farmer and the clerk kept arguing to no one's satisfaction. Paul Cameron wanted that story every single time he got to choose.

There were the stories of *Raggedy Ann and Andy; Doctor Doolittle*, who talked to the animals; *the Bobbsey Twins; Mary Poppins; Uncle Remus; Little Women* and, of course, all the fairy tales. Mother read dog stories like *Lad and Lassie* and horse stories like *Black Beauty, The Red Pony* and *My Friend Flicka*. She read about *Hans Brinker and the Silver Skates*, the story about a little boy who stuck his finger in the dike and saved Holland. Sometimes she would even read grownup books to us if she thought we would enjoy them. One such book was *Cheaper by the Dozen* about a family with twelve children. We did have many laughs and good conversations about that book.

Rudyard Kipling's stories like *How the Elephant got his Trunk* and *How the Camel Got His Hump* were set in exotic places with hard to pronounce names. They usually taught a lesson and they sometimes had poetry too, like, *The Camel's hump is an ugly lump which well you may see at the zoo; But uglier yet is the hump we get from having too little to do.*

My mother read poetry to us a lot—all kinds of poetry.

From Henry Wadsworth Longfellow we knew *Between the dark and the daylight, when the light is beginning to lower, comes a pause in the day's occupations that is known as the Children's Hour.*

That was our time.

We knew about *The Midnight Ride of Paul Revere: Listen, my children and you shall hear of the midnight ride of Paul Revere. On the eighteenth of*

April in seventy-five, hardly a man is now alive who remembers that famous day and year.

We knew about the *Village Blacksmith: Under the spreading chestnut tree, the village smithy stands; The smith, a mighty man is he with large and sinewy hands; And the muscles of his brawny arms are strong as iron bands.*

From Longfellow we also knew about Hiawatha and the Indian nations of the west: *By the shores of Gitchie Gumee, by the shining big sea water, At the doorway of his wigwam, in the pleasant summer morning, Hiawatha stood and waited.*

The United States was at war; the whole world was at war, just as the Indian Nations had been in the Song of Hiawatha when the Great Spirit chastised the Indian nations for being ungrateful for all their blessings, and for all their killing of one another. He told them: *I am weary of your quarrels; weary of your wars and bloodshed, weary of your prayers for vengeance, all your wrangling and dissensions; All your strength is in your union, all your danger is in discord; Therefore be at peace and henceforward, as brothers live together.*

Then the Great Spirit ordered them to: *Wash the war-paint from your faces, wash the blood-stains from your fingers, bury your war-clubs and your weapons. Break the red stone from this quarry, mold and make it into Peace-Pipes.*

And the Indian Nations did as the Great Spirit spoke.

I fervently wished the Nations of World War II could hear and do likewise.

We had the book *A Child's Garden of Verses* by Robert Louis Stevenson, and I knew practically all the poem in that book by heart.

How do you like to go up in a swing, up in the air so blue? Oh I do think it the pleasantest thing ever a child could do!

Up into the cherry tree, who should climb but little me? I held the trunk with both my hands and looked abroad on foreign lands.

Sally Ann Webb McPherson

I have a little shadow that goes in and out with me and what can be the use of him is more than I can see.

I saw you toss the kites on high and blow the birds about the sky; And all around I heard you pass, like ladies' skirts across the grass—O wind, a blowing all day long, O wind that sings so loud a song!

We had a book called *The Organ Grinder's Handbook* where I found a poem I especially liked: *Twenty Froggies went to school down beside a rushing pool. Twenty little coats of green, twenty vests all shiny clean…*

We did love the poems of James Whitcomb Riley when my mother read them! Not just anybody can read these poems because they are written sort of funny, in a dialect and language patterns not familiar to children in the South.

O The man in the moon has a crick in 'is back; Whee! Whim! Ain't you sorry for him? And a mole on his nose that is purple and black; And his eyes are so weak that they water and run. If he dares to dream even he looks at the sun, So he jes' dreams of the stars as the doctors advise… O the Raggedy Man! He works for Pa an' he's the goodest man you ever saw. He comes to our house every day, an' waters the horses, an' feeds um hay.

Our favorite James Whitcomb Riley poem was long and sort of scary: *Little Orphant Annie* comes to our house to stay, An' wash the cups and saucers up, an' brush the crumbs away; An' shoo the chickens off the porch, an' dust the hearth, an' sweep, An' make the fire, an' bake the bread, an' earn her board-an'-keep; An' all us other children, when the supper-things is done, We set around the kitchen fire an' has the mostest fun A-list'nin' to the witch-tales 'at Annie tells about, An' the gobble-uns'll git you ef you don't watch out.

Then "Orphant Annie" proceeds to tell about the fate of a little boy who wouldn't say his prayers, and a little girl who made fun of others and showed no respect for her elders. Then, it ends with this:

An' little Orphant Annie says, when the blaze is blue, An' the lamp-wick sputters, an' the wind goes woo-oo! An' you hear the crickets quit, an' the moon is gray, An the lightnin' bugs in dew is all squenched away, You better mind yer parunts an' yer teachers fond an' dear, An' churish them 'at loves you, an' dry the orphant's tear, An' he'p the pore an'needy ones 'at clusters all about, Er the Gobble-uns'll git you ef you don't watch out!

Whether it is Uncle Remus in the deep South of Georgia, or James Whitcomb Riley up North in Indiana, or Longfellow in Boston writing about western plains Indians, or Robert Louis Stevenson in England or Rudyard Kipling in exotic India and Africa, the stories and the language used to tell them are compelling and beautiful. The stories made us feel connected to people everywhere.

From my mother's reading, I learned to appreciate the beauty of spoken language— the choice and meaning of words, the way words sound, the cadence, the timing, the intensity or mellowness, the humor or pathos, the sheer delight in a story well-told.

I would rather hear a story or a poem or a song than read it, any day. I just wish everyone could read aloud like my mother.

The Radio

We had a small radio in the pantry. That is where Betty Harris, our maid and cook, who also lived with us, listened to the soap opera stories in the afternoon when she did the ironing. Betty and Daddy always discussed the stories when he got home. The pantry is where we listened to the evening news while Daddy fixed himself a bourbon and branch water.

In the small living room we had a large cabinet radio and phonograph player. That is where we listened to special broadcasts, like when President Roosevelt addressed the nation. That is where we listened to our favorite programs before we went to bed. Skippy liked *The Shadow* that had a tag line, "The Shadow knows…" We listened to *The Lone Ranger*. Those stories always ended with, "Who was that masked man?" We listened to Henry Aldrich, whose mother had an irritating way of calling him. She would shout, "Henry! Hennnrrrry Aldrich!" We listened to *The Life of Riley* that had a character—Digger O'Dell—who was an undertaker and who would exit his part of the show saying, "Well, I'd better be shoveling off."

I liked *The Jack Benny Show*. Jack Benny was funny and he was a tightwad penny pincher. The interesting characters on the show made jokes and poked fun at one another. They also sang. Dennis Day was an Irish tenor with a sweet, smooth voice. Phil Harris sang too, in a husky gravelly voice. The show was always entertaining. Sometimes we would lollygag on the floor to listen, spread out on our backs or lying on our bellies with our knees bent and our feet in the air. Sometimes we would set up a card table and put together a jigsaw puzzle while we listened; or if it were not our favorite program, we would sit on the sofa and look at books while we listened.

Sally Ann Webb McPherson

Childhood Diseases

In the 1940s, most children became ill with what were referred to as "childhood diseases" because they typically affected children. For most of the diseases, if you had the illness, you were immune to what caused it and you did not get it again. That's why adults did not often get them.

My brothers and I had all the childhood diseases, and when one of us got sick, soon we were all sick. You could count on it.

There were two kinds of measles: the red measles and the German measles. Measles gave you a fever and a headache, and all you wanted to do was sleep. It hurt to lift your head off the pillow. Measles made you break out in a red rash that itched. When you had the measles, you had to pull shades down in your bedroom to keep out bright lights, and you were not allowed to read. If you got in bright light or strained your eyes, it could affect your vision for the rest of your life. You could even go blind. Once when we had the measles, my mother got them too because she had never had this kind of measles when she was a child. Measles make adults even sicker than they make children. My mother had to go to the hospital in Durham, and we were extremely worried about her.

Chicken Pox was a lot like measles—you felt awful. Instead of a red rash that itched, you broke out in little sores that itched *and* hurt. You were not supposed to touch or scratch the sores because if you did, it would leave a scar sort of like the Small Pox scar that we all had because we had been vaccinated against the Small Pox. Small Pox was considered a real killer disease, so we were glad the vaccine protected us from it. Chicken Pox was not supposed to be as bad, but it was bad enough, and we certainly did not want those scars all over our faces and bodies.

Mumps not only make you sick, mumps make you ugly. Mumps is a disease that affects the glands, usually the glands in your neck, just under your jawbone, in front of your ears. These glands swell up horribly, making your neck look like it is part of your face and everything is sort of square. Mumps hurt like crazy all the time; you run a fever and sleep a lot. When we had the mumps and the boys were beginning to feel better, they got to wrestling with each other. Paul Cameron kicked Skippy in the groin—that's the area between his legs, near his penis—and oh my! In addition to having the mumps in his neck, Skip had them in his groin too and he was in severe pain. It was a long time before he recovered.

Paul Cameron was the only one of us that got the childhood disease Whooping Cough. He coughed and coughed really violently, and it sounded as if he could not breathe at all. We were scared.

There were other diseases that worried parents a lot.

Polio, short for poliomyelitis, was the horrible disease that had crippled the President of the United States. It affected lots of children as well. Thankfully, I did not personally know anyone who had polio. It somehow affected muscles, and that is how it crippled people. Children who had polio sometimes had to live in a big metal chamber called an iron lung because they did not have the muscle power to breathe on their own. In the summer, parents made their children stay inside and rest after lunch so as not to get overheated or overtired and risk getting polio.

Rocky Mountain Spotted Fever was a disease you got from ticks. Each summer we got a shot to prevent us from getting this disease. We played outside constantly where there were ticks. Especially after picking blackberries, my mother would examine us all over for ticks. It didn't take long to examine the boys because in the 1940s boys had extremely short hair—GI haircuts—named after the soldiers whose hair was practically shaven when they entered the Army. It took a longer time to look through my long, thick hair. I never knew why this disease was called Rocky Mountain Spotted Fever. We lived in North Carolina and not even in the mountains.

We also got a shot to prevent Typhoid Fever. That shot always resulted in swelling and redness and fever at the place where the shot was given. If the shot hurt that bad, I sure did not want to get Typhoid Fever.

Teen Age Heart Throb

The singer Frank Sinatra was the rage and the heart-throb of popular music!

My friend Joan Forrest and Skippy's friend Bobby Forrest had teenage sisters who were best friends, Betsy and Phyllis. One time I was at Joan's house when the teenagers came running and giggling and squealing into the house. They went straight to the living room where the phonograph player was. They were so excited because they had a new record to play—it was Frank Sinatra's latest hit song. Betsy and Phyllis draped themselves over a chair and sofa and played that record over and over. Joan and I just rolled our eyes.

I would be a teenager myself, and Elvis Presley would be "The King" before I would understand the girls' fascination with Frank Sinatra.

Sally Ann Webb McPherson

Adults Played, Too

In addition to visiting and sitting on porches telling stories and having cocktails, adults in those days played at other things, too.

In the fall, college football was the passion. Adults listened to games on the radio and went to games on nearby campuses. We lived a short drive from Chapel Hill, Durham and Raleigh—home to the University of North Carolina, Duke University and North Carolina State University. Everybody had a favorite team. My parents and my Aunt Annie would go to home games at Kenan Stadium at Carolina. They would pack a picnic to share with others before the game. If the food was supposed to be hot, they would heat it and wrap the container in layers and layers and layers of newspaper to insulate it and keep it warm.

After the games, people would come to our house to rehash the games, talk about the standings and have supper. My mother would have made a one-dish meal like Brunswick stew, ham and navy bean soup, or chili. She usually had made fresh home-baked bread to go with the meal; she cut it in big, thick chunks. Our maid called mother's homemade bread "vitamin bread."

Alice Webb's Brunswick Stew

1 5-6 lb. hen

2 lbs. pork

½ stick butter

2 quarts tomatoes—peeled, quartered and packed

6 onions, chopped

½ teaspoon each, sugar, salt and pepper

1 quart fresh (or frozen) butter beans

1 quart riced or mashed potatoes

¼ cup ketchup

½ bottle Worcestershire sauce

8 ears white corn or 1 quart frozen white corn

2 pieces crisp bacon

Cook hen and pork slowly. When cool, shred the meat. [Pull apart with two forks.] In heavy pot, put meat with all broth, seasonings, onions and tomatoes. Cook slowly for 2 hours. Add butterbeans and cook 1 hour. Add corn and cook ½ hour. Then, add Worcestershire, ketchup and potatoes. Simmer. Adjust seasoning to taste.

In winter, if it snowed the adults would go sledding. After we children went to bed, our parents would take the sleds and meet other adults over at the hill by St. Matthew's Church—a really good, steep sledding hill with a long level place at the bottom to coast to a stop. That road would be closed to traffic. The adults would build a bonfire and have a really good time. I always thought it would be fun to go with them because we children never got to close a street or have a bonfire when we went sledding; however, these outings were strictly for grownups.

Sometimes the adults would play poker. I liked it when they played at our house because I would sneak down the stairs and be very quiet and watch. Both men and women played, sitting around our big dining room table—some players would stand around the table watching or go to the kitchen to keep refreshments coming. They would laugh and tease one another. The adults played poker at other people's homes, too; sometimes only the men played.

My mother belonged to a book club. All of the club members bought a different book, and once a month the ladies would meet and talk about the books and swap books. That way, they did not have to buy all of the books. They took turns having book club at different club members' homes. There were always refreshments and talk about things other than the books as well.

Mother also belonged to a bridge club. When the ladies played bridge at our house, there were card tables set in both living rooms and my mother bought prizes for the ladies with the best scores. They would rotate around so they didn't play all the time with the same partners or opponents. They always enjoyed delicious refreshments too.

My mother once made an extraordinary dessert for bridge club. The dessert was made of meringues—egg whites whipped and whipped until they are stiff and thick, seasoned with almond, loaded with sugar and then baked slowly on brown paper in a barely warm oven until they are dry and a light beige color. For the family, my mother would make them in globs with a hollow. Then she put ice cream in the hollow and topped that with strawberries and whipped cream—sort of like strawberry shortcake, except with meringues instead of cake.

For bridge club she made the hollowed-out little globs and shaped one end sort of like a ducktail. Then, on brown paper, she drew outlines like a swan's neck and head and filled that with the egg white before baking it. She used a toothpick to hook the neck and head piece to the glob with the tail and…magically, there was a three dimensional swan to fill with ice cream, strawberries and whip cream. Those swans were the prettiest dessert I had ever seen!

My parents would also play bridge with just one other couple sometimes, sitting by the fireplace or on the side porch. My grandmother and my Aunt Annie liked to play bridge too.

Meringues

Having egg whites at room temperature is essential for successful meringues.

1 cup sugar

8 egg whites—at room temperature

1/8 teaspoon salt

Beat egg whites until stiff. Slowly add sugar, one teaspoon at a time, beating the egg whites constantly. Continue beating for several minutes after the last sugar has been added. The mixture will become shiny and thick and will stand in peaks.

Add:

1 teaspoon vanilla

Fold in:

½ cup sugar (scant)

Place large spoonfuls on a baking sheet that is covered with brown paper. Press each dollop in center with the back of a large spoon to form a nest. Bake very slowly, @ 225° for 45 minutes. Turn oven off and let meringues dry in oven with door cracked open for 10 minutes.

May be made several days in advance. Makes twelve, 3" meringues. Serve with a scoop of ice cream topped with sliced strawberries (or other fresh fruit) and whipped cream.

One man in our town had a special way to have fun. Dr. Bryan Roberts would close his office when the circus came to Raleigh and go work at the circus. The story was that when he was just a boy, he ran away to join the circus and never stopped loving it.

People entertained in their homes a lot in those days. For Sunday dinner and holiday meals we often had guests filling our big table and many children at a separate table. My parents would sometimes have dinner parties without children.

Parties that didn't include dinner were my favorite. My parents would have parties at Christmas, a birthday or something special—sometimes just because it was their turn to entertain. The house would be decorated with fresh flowers and greenery in every room. There were all kinds of finger foods served hot and cold on silver trays and crystal plates. The party would include a big silver punchbowl with fruit punch or eggnog and cocktails.

For special parties, my parents had special help. Living in our town was a beautiful colored woman named Marinda McPherson, who would help at parties. Marinda would wear a black uniform with a stiff white ruffled apron like in the movies, and she would help serve food and drink. But the highlight of every such party was when Marinda would sing. Not only was Marinda beautiful, when she sang, you could hardly breathe while listening to her. She had been to music school in New York City and had a trained voice. Guests listened in awe and utter silence.

Once I went to the movies at night to see a movie starring a beautiful colored woman named Lena Horne, who sang "Stormy Weather." Marinda could have been a movie star—she was just as pretty—and I thought she sang better than Lena Horne.

Once there was Christmas caroling at the courthouse at night with candles; people from all the church choirs participated. Marinda sang a solo, *Oh Holy Night.* It was absolutely the most beautiful sound I ever heard. I always think of her when I hear that song, and it is my favorite Christmas carol.

Music was always an important part of parties. Sometimes people would gather around our piano in the back hall while I would sit on the stairs to watch and listen. My favorite was when Dr. Joe Beard would play and sing. Dr. Beard wasn't a regular doctor; he was a research doctor who worked in laboratories at Duke Hospital. Dr. Beard played guitar and knew how to play everything from old-timey to modern—folk songs, spirituals, popular songs, cowboy songs and Broadway musicals, big band renditions, even hymns and patriotic songs. Before we children went to bed, he would play *Froggy Went a Courtin.'* He would sing the verse and everyone else would sing the "Uh Humm, Uh Humm" part. *Froggy went 'a courting' and he did ride, Uh humm, Uh Humm...Froggy went 'a courting' and he did ride, sword and a pistol by his side, Uh humm, Uh Humm...*

It was a silly song with silly lyrics and was so much fun!

Another silly song that he played especially for the children was *I went to the animal fair, the birds and the beasts were there. The big baboon, by the light of the moon was combing his auburn hair. The monkey, he got drunk and fell on the elephant's trunk. The elephant sneezed and fell on his knees and that was the end of the Monkeyty-Monk The Monkeyty-Monkeyty-Monkeyty-Monk!*

Adults went to movies, but not the Saturday afternoon cowboy movies, and to plays in Raleigh and Durham. They went swimming and fishing out in the country at Dr. Roberts' pond where he had a cabin. They would also play board games like checkers and chess—they even played checkers downtown at the hardware store. My mother liked to work crossword puzzles. Sometimes adults would put together picture puzzles and let us children help.

It was nice to know that you did not have to stop playing and having fun just because you grew up.

Smoking

Most adults I knew smoked. Those that did not smoke cigarettes smoked pipes or cigars. Cousin Paul smoked a pipe, and I loved the smell of pipe tobacco. I liked to smell cigars too, but I thought cigarettes just smelled dirty. My mother smoked Pall Malls (pronounced *Pell Mell*) and my daddy smoked Camels. Advertisements for Camels stated, "I'd walk a mile for a Camel." "L.S.M.F.T—Lucky Strike means fine tobacco" touted the Lucky Strike brand. Chesterfield cigarettes advertised "21 fine tobaccos."

People smoked just about everywhere except in church. In the home, ashtrays were in every room, and dinner tables were set with little individual ashtrays. Businesses set ashtrays beside the cash registers and ashtrays were on restaurant tables and counters. Cars, equipped with lighters and ashtrays, smelled of stale smoke.

My mother frowned at women walking around smoking—she thought that was tacky. I did not know much about smoking etiquette, but I did observe that gentlemen usually asked ladies, "Do you mind if I smoke?" When the lady said no, the gentleman would offer her a cigarette and she would either take it, or reach for her own brand. Then, with cigarettes in their mouths, the man would pull out a lighter or match, lean into the woman, and light her cigarette before lighting his own. In real life, this looked just as romantic as it did in the movies.

People carried cigarette lighters or matchbooks in their pockets and purses. Ladies' lighters were smaller than those carried by men, and they were sometimes silver with initials engraved on them. A heavy, ornate, sterling silver lighter beside a silver ashtray graced our living room coffee table.

Popular music memorialized the smoking culture with songs like *Smoke, Smoke, Smoke That Cigarette,* a comical song acknowledging how the need to smoke interrupts life and even death "when you smoke yourself to death"; and romantic songs like *Smoke Gets in Your Eyes* and *These Foolish Things* such as "A cigarette that bears a lipstick's traces."

Many businesses gave away matchbooks. Sometimes the matchbook cover advertised their own business; sometimes it advertised another business, product or service.

I did think it odd that while adults smoked profusely, they admonished us children not to smoke—telling us emphatically, "*Smoking will stunt your growth!*"

Sally Ann Webb McPherson

School Year 1944-1945—A Difficult Year

I was five years old in 1944 and about to become aware of age discrimination.

My best friend was Buck Roberts, who lived across the street and was closer to my age than any of my other friends—one year minus fourteen days older than I. That is why in September 1944, when Buck was six years old and I was five years old, he got to go to school and I did not. My mother tried to register me, but the school was firm and they would not admit me.

I already knew how to read and do addition and subtraction. I could count to one hundred by ones, by twos, by fives and by tens—you had to know that to play hide and go seek. And anybody knows once you can count to one hundred you can count to anything!

My brother Skip had trouble reading and writing. He would see letters backwards then would read and write them backwards. This problem of Skip's had a name; it was called dyslexia. Anyway, he needed lots of help. My mother would spend hours and hours with him every day, pointing to the words and helping him with his reading and writing. He even wrote letters backwards because that was the way he saw them.

Dyslexia

The term dyslexia was first coined by a German ophthalmologist, Rudolph Berlin, in 1887. In 1896, a British physician published a description on this reading-specific learning disorder. Dyslexia is characterized by the inability to recognize and relate to written symbols. It is not related to intelligence.

During Skippy's first and second grade, I was in a plaster leg cast because of my osteomyelitis, so I sat in on the lessons. Skip would try so hard and get so frustrated. That is why I did not laugh even though I thought that it was really funny when once he got D-O-G and G-O-D mixed up.

I did not have dyslexia, so I learned to read, even though my mother was not teaching me. I could complete all of Skippy's assignments and read first-and second-grade books. I could recite the Boy Scout Creed long before Skippy could, but they would not let me join the Boy Scouts either.

My parents considered a private kindergarten in Durham for me. There was a war going on and gas was rationed, so that wasn't possible. I was really lonesome.

One fine fall day when the sun was bright and the leaves on all the trees were absolutely ablaze with color, I had a brilliant idea. I picked a beautiful assortment of leaves from all the different trees and arranged them just so. Then I walked the block down to the school and climbed the steps to the elementary classrooms. I knew which room Buck Roberts was in. I knocked on the door and told his teacher I had brought her a present. She invited me in and thanked me for the beautiful bouquet. But alas, she would not let me stay. I had to return home. Soon, my parents had lots of sympathy because everyone in town heard the story about their daughter who wanted to go to school.

My parents did their best to keep me busy, entertained and learning. My mother would take me shopping and visiting with her. She would read to me and play jacks with me. My daddy would let me help him in the garden. He taught me the names of plants and flowers and how to identify trees by their leaves and barks. We planted seeds in the greenhouse and transplanted them to the garden.

I raked leaves with Jim Mayo, our yard man, and he gave me rides in the wheelbarrow.

I stretched the patience of Betty Harris. Betty was strictly business. She never physically disciplined me, but when I would get on her very last nerve, she would march me out to the backyard and most carefully select a switch—usually a long, slender, willowy branch from a forsythia bush. She would hold that switch with her right hand and dramatically strip all the leaves, right down to the tip, in one fell swoop with her left hand. *Zip!* Then she would test the switch in the air—*Swisssss…swissssss…Swissssssss!!!* It was enough to scare the freckles off this little redhead! I would surely find something else to do quickly.

Betty Harris did make the world's best lemon meringue pie! Talk about "melt in your mouth" and a happy overload for the taste buds! It was more than delicious.

Betty Harris' Lemon Meringue Pie

6 eggs

1 tablespoon flour stirred into

½ cup sugar

juice and zest of 1 large lemon or 2 regular lemons [1/3 cup +]

½ cup sugar

Separate eggs. Beat yolks until light. Add sugar, flour, juice and zest. Cook over low heat in double boiler until thick and creamy. Cool.

Beat egg whites until very stiff. Add ½ cup sugar gradually while beating. Fold ½ of the meringue into the yolk mixture, leaving ½ for the top of the pie.

Fill partially cooked pie crust with yolk mixture and top with remaining meringue. Seal edges. Bake slowly in medium oven.

In November, the United States of America had an election and my president, Franklin D. Roosevelt, was re-elected. I was glad. My family was not.

There was a little colored girl from the country named Joyce who sometimes came to play with me that winter. We would play happily, building things or playing games. Joyce, like me, would rather do that than play with dolls.

I remember once my mother took me across town to play with my friend Margaret Ray. Margaret Ray had a sister Martha just one year younger than we were and a baby brother named Ted. When my mother picked me up, she asked me what we did. I told her we had a really good time—we built a stable and a manger and we were playing *Mary, Joseph and the Baby Jesus*. But we had to stop because baby Ted would not stay in the manger like he was supposed to do.

I spent a lot of time by myself. I would climb to the very tippy-top of the magnolia tree and think. I would explore. I would make up songs.

I loved making up songs, and I especially liked doing it when there was no one to hear them or make fun of them. Instead of songs, they were probably more like Winnie the Pooh's little hums that he would hum to himself like his honey song: *"Isn't it funny how a bear likes honey? Buzz. Buzz. It's funny, but he does"*; or his stoutness exercise song *"...Tra-la-la, rum-tum-tiddle-um-tum"*; or, like my favorite Pooh hum where he hums: *A fly cannot bird, but a bird can fly!"*

Once, I was playing on the sidewalk out by our driveway when boys from the high school came along. They were probably from West Hillsborough because I did not know them. They hollered ugly names at me. When I tried to go home, they chased me and said they were going to put dog-shit on me. I ran, but they caught me and they did indeed rub fresh, moist, stinky dog-shit in my hair. I cried. When my mother was washing my hair, I think she cried too.

I got over feeling bad faster than my mother did. She was upset because they did that to me, but I knew they were just mean boys who were not raised right.

That incident, however, resulted in my getting in trouble myself.

I kind of liked the word dog-shit. We had always called it "poop," but "dog-shit" was just so much more expressive. I began to look for opportunities to say "dog-shit." I was told that people in polite company did not talk like that, and I was told not to say it. Then I was told if I ever said it again, I would have my mouth washed out with soap. I simply could not resist that juicy forbidden fruit of a word, "dog-shit." And then, there I was perched on the kitchen table with my daddy standing in front of me with a wet washcloth and green Palmolive soap. Yuk! It was awful and I choked. After that, I was careful to use language that was acceptable in polite company.

For my birthday that year, my aunts from Raleigh brought fabulous refreshments for my party. The cake was white cake with white icing formed into the shape of a lamb. There were white, fluffy coconut flakes all over the lamb to make him look fuzzy-wuzzy. He was almost too cute to eat. They also brought raspberry sherbet. I had never in my life imagined anything so elegant as raspberry sherbet.

For that birthday, when I was finally six years old, I got the best birthday present I have ever received—including before that birthday and for all the ones to follow.

Our yard man, Jim Mayo, baked me a cake. My mother said Jim had baked it in a wood-burning stove, a feat which in itself was amazing. This was no ordinary cake. I still have never seen anything like it ever again. It was sort of a pound cake, baked in an ornate cast iron mold; it was about ten inches high and weighed a ton. It was golden colored and it was, to me, the most beautiful thing ever seen. In addition, it was purely delicious.

I really appreciated the lamb cake and my aunts' going to all the trouble and caring enough to bring that adorable thing from Raleigh, but that lamb cake could not be compared to Jim's cake. Thinking about Jim's cake warms my heart to this day.

When I went to Bible School and heard the story of the widow's mite, where Jesus praised the widow who did not have much to give, but gave what she had, I understood why it was so special to me. Jim loved me and he gave me what he had; he baked me that magnificent cake. I am still grateful and humbled when I remember that cake.

The Ringling Brothers and Barnum & Bailey Circus, "The Greatest Show on Earth," came to Raleigh in the spring of 1945. Our family went to see it. Skippy got out of school to go. It was a really big deal. I did not know what to expect, but I most certainly was looking forward to seeing elephants.

There were so many people and so much was happening. Before we got to the Big Top—that was the humongous tent where the circus performed—we passed by wagons and tents buzzing with activity. This was the area of the sideshows. Each show had people standing outside telling us what was inside and trying to entice us to come in. Amazing feats of daring, the fat lady, sword swallowers, dancing girls, unfortunate people billed as freaks—all beckoned us to step right up and go inside! We did step right up and go inside one called the hall of mirrors. It was really funny! There were trick mirrors that would make you appear to be extremely tall and skinny, or fat, fat, fat, or just misshapen.

Inside the Big Top, the activity continued before the actual show started. People were selling popcorn and Crackerjacks. A band played music. The clowns were out and about—all kinds of clowns doing silly things that made us laugh. When we were finally in our seats, a really sad-looking clown passed by us. Then the people in our section were laughing. The clown had gone to the spot behind me and my Aunt Annie and pretended our hair was afire and he was warming his hands. My Aunt Annie had red hair like me and she was really pretty. That clown made the most of it. He would pretend to leave and then come back and warm his hands some more. He stayed there clowning around for a long time. I learned later that the clown's name was Emmett Kelly, an enormously famous person, one of the world's best known entertainers.

There was at least one band playing happy, energetic music all the time. When it was time for the show to begin, a parade of performers and animals circled the three rings where the acts would be performed. The horses and elephants with colorful, sparkling costumes draped over them carried people in brilliant costumes; the circus people stood up on the animals and waved. Beautiful tigers and lions paced in gilded, fancy wagons. I didn't know tigers and lions were so huge in real life. The clowns were in the parade, prancing or walking on stilts, riding on tricycles or jam-packed into funny little cars.

After the parade, the show began and within seconds, there was just too much going on to keep track of all the acts, even though there was a Ring Master announcing the acts and telling about them. The music went perfectly with each act so when it changed, you knew to look for a different act about to start. I liked the acrobats gliding through the air on the flying trapeze—they were so graceful—but it was a bit scary too. My favorites were all the animal acts and, of those, my most favorite were the elephants.

The circus was truly "The Greatest Show on Earth," and we had so much fun!

We were so excited and eager to tell everybody about the circus when we got home, but then a sad thing happened.

Daddy turned on the pantry radio to listen to the evening news. H. V. Kaltenborn reported that the President of the United States had died suddenly at Warm Springs, Georgia.

I was passionately patriotic and Franklin Delano Roosevelt was my

President. I listened to the news with H.V. Kaltenborn or Edward R. Murrow. I watched the newsreels every Saturday when we went to the movies. I thought President Roosevelt was handsome. I liked the way he talked, the words he chose, and his booming voice. We shared a physical infirmity and were confined to a wheelchair—he all the time, me part time. I was personally inspired by all he could do from that chair. He was Commander-in-Chief for all the soldiers, sailors and Marines; he met with Winston Churchill, our ally in the war; he spoke to the nation and tried to help us understand what was going on in the war and what was required of those of us who were not fighting the war.

My family did not share my admiration and patriotic passion for the President of the United States, but I accepted that. What cut me to the core, what knocked all the joy of the circus day from my mind, and what destroyed the well-being within me was that my daddy was glad that my President was dead.

I was devastated. I was crushed. I was so sad. I left the pantry where my daddy and I always listened to the news and went out into the cold and rainy backyard. My eyes filled with tears. I walked down to the end of the driveway and had myself a really good cry. I did not want to go back to the house. I felt alienated. Mr. Roosevelt, the President of the United States, was the first whom I loved to die, and I had no one to mourn with me.

How, or why, can a newly turned six-year-old be so aware and so opinionated? I don't know, but I was.

The President of the United States had died.

When President Roosevelt died, his Vice President, Harry S. Truman, became President of the United States. My parents did not like Mr. Truman either.

I became disillusioned with politics after President Roosevelt died; however, I did become briefly interested in the election of 1948. I followed it in the newsreels at the Saturday movies, but not as passionately as I had followed Mr. Roosevelt. Mr. Truman was in a close race for president with Thomas Dewey. The newsreels showed Mr. Truman traveling across the country by train and making compelling speeches from the back of the train when it would stop. The crowds looked huge.

On the night of the election, the race was still extremely close. H.V. Kaltenborn was on the radio reporting as each state's election results came in. I woke up and came downstairs to check on the election. Daddy was satisfied and went to bed when Mr. Kaltenborn projected that Dewey would be the winner. The next morning, the news reports were that President Truman had been elected! He had won more states and substantially more electoral votes than Mr. Dewey. The newsreels on the following Saturday showed a picture of a smiling President Truman holding a Chicago newspaper with a huge headline: *Dewey Defeats Truman.* This is surely a lesson in "Don't count your chickens before they hatch!"

President Truman favored civil rights for negroes and integrated the United States Armed Services, providing equality of treatment and opportunity for colored people in the U.S. Army, Navy, Air Force and Marines. I thought that was only right.

Before Harry S. Truman, with no middle name, became well known, our family had a James H. Webb. This cousin had assumed the H because there were so many James Webbs in North Carolina at the time that it was confusing. When James H. Webb's daughter was to be married, his wife insisted it was not proper to put just an initial on the wedding invitations. James H. Webb said, "Well, you can take your pick. It could be Hogg, or it could be Hillsborough." The invitations were engraved with simply "Mr. and Mrs. James Webb."

That spring when I was banned from school, like other springs, my daddy's garden was scheduled to be on the Hillsborough Garden Tour, when many people from Durham, Raleigh, Chapel Hill and other places would come to Hillsborough to spend the day and tour the beautiful gardens. My daddy's garden was always spectacular.

Daddy's vegetable gardens consisted of a series of neat, squared-off, raised beds with walkways between them. The vegetables were planted in straight rows with markers for the vegetables growing there. It was neat and organized—highly regimented.

Daddy's flower gardens, on the other hand, did not know a straight line. My daddy had studied horticulture, botany and landscape design at the University of North Carolina, and he was the first Director of the Duke Gardens in Durham. His home gardens revealed the same care in design and artistic talent exhibited at the Duke Gardens.

Color, texture and foliage rioted there, seemingly unorganized, but they were not. Short, low plants and flowers like cow slips, candy tuff, forget-me-nots, pansies, ageratum and even peanuts with small yellow flowers grew along the edges of the borders. Medium height plants came next—plants like tulips, jonquils and narcissus, hyacinths, and crocus came in the spring. Plants like geraniums, snap dragons, petunias, bachelor buttons, delphinium and larkspur bloomed all summer; and chrysanthemums, asters and dahlias bloomed in the fall. Then came taller bushes and shrubs like azaleas, gardenias, camellias, peonies, forsythia and spiraea.

Spiraea flowers were white and lacy, and they attracted a huge, black bumble bee. We children called it "the black bumble bee bush" until I learned what its name was.

Behind the bushes stood trees like fir, lilac, redbud, dogwood, Japanese magnolia and white ash. These trees separated the front garden from the back garden and provided a backdrop and height to both.

There was nothing purely straight; the garden curved gently, ever so slightly. The plants all jumbled together. It was gorgeous—lots of color, texture and tapestry at every level. The front border was pleasantly visible from the side porch of our house. It had a flagstone pathway in the center. At the northern edge Daddy planted an ash tree. At the southern edge a narrow passage connected the front garden to the back garden near the southern linden tree, a relatively famous tree because it had been photographed for the cover of a national magazine. Nobody in Hillsborough knew until the magazine was published.

Duke Gardens

Often spoken of as "the crown jewel of Duke University," Duke Gardens occupies fifty-five acres in the heart of Duke's west campus, adjacent to Duke University Medical Center. The Sarah P. Duke Gardens provide a place where people of all backgrounds and ages come for beauty, education, horticulture, solitude, discovery, study, renewal and inspiration.

The gardens are recognized as one of the premier public gardens in the United States, renowned both for landscape design and the quality of horticulture, each year attracting more than 300,000 visitors from all over the world.

From the web site at http://www.hr.duke.edu/dukegardens/

The back garden was a narrow oval shape with a magnificent Jerusalem pear tree in the center. That tree was sure-enough splendid in the springtime with a mass of white flowers, but I do not know why it was called a pear tree because it never had pears. The same types of plants appearing in the front borders also built the borders in the back garden.

Sally Ann in her Cosmos Garden

The gardens displayed daisies and many varieties of daylilies, but I had observed that the best place to see and pick daisies was on Saint Mary's Road between Aunt Eliza's and the Kirkland's. In summer, the roadside was jammed with them, courtesy of Mother Nature. Masses of yellow daylilies grew in the ditch on the Durham Road, just as pretty as any in a garden. I remembered from Bible School that Jesus Christ had said, *"Consider the lilies of the field, they toil not, neither do they spin..."* These lilies grew wild in a ditch, but I was sure that they were indeed arrayed more beautifully than Solomon in all his glory, just as Jesus had said.

Daddy did not have roses in these flower gardens. Roses had a separate bed all to themselves in the back yard.

That spring, when I was not in school, I helped Daddy with the flower garden preparation. We weeded, we pruned, we cultivated. I was really into gardening. I especially enjoyed being in the greenhouse—it had a distinct smell, like warm earth and life. Daddy usually had an orchid or two blooming there, hanging from overhead pipes. There were clay pots in all sizes and plants growing at different stages. It was great. In the greenhouse, Daddy started plants from seed in pots or wooden flats and then would transplant them to the garden.

It intrigued me how when we plant seeds and watch every day to see if they have germinated, when the first little green sprout stands up, there would be a part of the seed casing hanging onto the first two leaves that appeared. When that casing fell off, then the plant would begin to mature to the kind of plant it was meant to be. Daddy said those first two little leaves are called the cotyledon, a mighty big word for me.

One fine spring day, in the oval of the back garden, just after the passage through from the front garden to the back garden, I chopped up the grass and planted my own garden for the Garden Tour! It was an approximately 2 x 4 foot rectangle—no curves, all right angles. After checking the directions on the package, I planted *cosmos*, a seed packet I had purchased myself at The Corner Drug Store with my own money. Cosmos are a form of daisy, but in a myriad of pastel colors. We did not have any cosmos in the garden and we had no cosmos seeds growing in the greenhouse.

At first my daddy was furious; then he laughed and let my contribution remain. My garden was a highlight of the Garden Tour! I think that is because Southerners have a sense of humor and also because the cosmos were so very pretty, even if they were in a squared-off little patch where they should not have been.

Spring passed without my getting into too much more trouble. I, my parents and all of Hillsborough had survived. Summer came and again there were lots of children to share in adventures, explorations, sports and games; or to do a whole lot of nothing, like lying on our backs attributing shapes to clouds, or on our bellies searching for four-leaf clovers, or picking dandelions, making wishes and blowing all the puffy white seeds off the stem…. Life was good.

Now, I was six and I could go to school next year.

School—Finally, At Last!

In September 1945, I was finally allowed to go to school—age six, plus seven months. I was so excited! My parents were probably happier to see that day than I was. My mother took my picture.

Hillsborough had one school. It was a block from our driveway. Of course, it was red brick. North Carolina had a lot of red clay. That red brick school contained grade one through grade twelve. However, there were two buildings, connected by a covered, heated and ventilated hallway. We had one principal, one auditorium, one cafeteria. In the western-most building was the principal's office, the auditorium and the high school classrooms. In the eastern-most building were the elementary classrooms with the cafeteria in the basement.

Both buildings had high steps up to the front doors, wide hallways with wooden floors and high ceilings. The school janitor would sprinkle oiled sawdust in the hallways and sweep the floors with a wide push broom. The oiled sawdust had a pungent odor. The floors gleamed.

Classrooms also had wooden floors and high ceilings with big blackboards on two walls. The chalk and erasers also had a particular smell; the chalk dust made me sneeze. High windows stretched all the way to the ceiling along one wall. Teachers operated the windows with a long pole. Brass hardware loops were used to lock the windows and to raise and lower them. The long poles had an iron ball-shaped piece affixed to one end that fitted into the loops and a hook on the other end. The teachers could raise the windows from the bottom, or they could lower them from the top with those long poles. Remember—no air conditioning!

On the hill behind the school—up many steps, were the football field and baseball field. Across the street from the front of the high school, on the southwest corner, was the gymnasium where the school teams, and we children, played basketball.

We saw the Harlem Globetrotters play basketball in that gymnasium in Hillsborough, North Carolina, in the segregated South, in the 1940s. No one thought it odd that all these white people paid money, took their children, and filled the gymnasium to see these magnificent colored athletes and entertainers. The Harlem Globetrotters indeed trotted, but they also danced, passed, balanced, juggled and spun the ball; they dribbled and shot with grace, extraordinary coordination and tremendous skill. What a show it was! I wondered if the colored people got to see them.

To the east of the school the playground spread across a half acre or so, with a jungle gym, two kinds of swings and see-saws. One kind of swing was the traditional sit-on swing—you pumped or someone pushed you to go higher and higher; the other type of swing was what I would call a hang-on swing—you held on and ran faster and faster, lifting yourself off the ground. I guess it was designed to build upper body strength. All of the playground equipment was metal and made creaking, banging and clanking sounds—it was a noisy place!

When the weather was warm, boys would draw circles in the red clay under the maple trees at the front of the school and play marbles while waiting for the bell to ring calling us to class. To ensure they had a true circle, the boys employed two sticks and a length of brown twine tied to each stick. They would poke one stick where they wanted the center of the circle to be; then they would stretch the twine taut and proceed to pull it around the stick in the center to scratch a line in the clay and form the circumference of a perfect circle.

At last, I was enrolled in school and was assigned to Miss Annie Cameron's first grade class. Miss Annie was a cousin of my daddy's and also my Sunday School teacher. She had also been my daddy's first grade teacher. It was fine to call her "Miss Annie" because everyone in town called her "Miss Annie."

I loved school! I loved reading circle, practicing writing, and doing math. But certainly, the best part of school was all the children and new friends I had never met before.

There were also some mean students. Once, before school, several boys surrounded me and began a taunting chant.

Red, Red, Red on the head.
I'd rather be dead than have red on my head.

Lucky for me that by first grade, I had decided that having red on my head wasn't so bad. I thought my Aunt Annie was beautiful and I noticed how men affectionately called her Red, flirted with her and teased her.

However, having red hair was at once a burden and a blessing. People commented on it; many wanted to touch it for good luck. They would ask, "Where did you get your beautiful red hair?" I thought that was the dumbest question in the world! Neither of my parents had red hair; neither of my brothers had red hair. Aunt Annie and Cousin Gertrude were the only living redheads in our family, but I did learn that many dead ancestors had red hair. To make a point, Grandfather Paul Cameron had written in a letter, "As sure as my head is red…."

My red hair was heavy and thick. Following a shampoo, my mother would rinse my hair with a little bit of vinegar in a glass of water. That would make it possible to comb through my hair without tangled "rats' nests." On Saturday nights, sometimes my mother would roll my hair in rags so that I would have curls for church on Sunday. Most of the time, my hair was in pigtails—my mother called them French braids. When she braided my hair, Mother pulled so tightly that I swore it raised my eyebrows. Betty Harris said French braiding was what colored people called plaiting, and I observed that was true.

In first grade, I soon became good friends with a fellow classmate, Sidney Ann Sims, who was smart and pretty with long brown pigtails. Sidney Ann and I would walk to my house for lunch. We would fix Campbell's soup or pork n' beans from a can, or Betty Harris would make us a sandwich. Once, our mothers even bought the same fabric and used the same pattern to make us dresses alike.

Sidney Ann's mother was pretty, with soft brown eyes and dark brown curly hair. Her daddy looked just like Bing Crosby, the singer and actor, and wore a hat like Bing's, tilted over one eye. Sidney Ann had an older sister and a darling baby sister that we liked to dress up and take for walks in her stroller.

Sidney Ann lived in the mill village and both of her parents worked at Eno Cotton Mill. When I would sleep over at her house, we would carry buckets of water from a pump down the street to her house. Sometimes, we would carry slop jars down the street to empty and clean them. She even had an icebox with real ice in it.

Hilda and Sylvia Strayhorn were new friends in my class. I had lots of cousins, but Hilda and Sylvia were the only "double first cousins" I knew—this was an entirely new term for me. Their fathers were brothers and their mothers were sisters. Once, I visited their grandparents who lived right in town and had a cow. They let me try to milk the cow. I was not successful, but it was fun trying, and the patient cow was a good sport.

Aside from the new friends, the highlight of first grade was a field trip. We took a hike up the hill behind the school, picking plants and studying how seeds are dispersed. We discovered fluffy dandelions whose seeds fly away; beggar lice, sand spurs and Spanish needles that stick to shoes and clothes to catch a ride somewhere else; maple tree seeds called "keys" that flutter and fly on the wind. It was all oh so interesting.

When we returned to class, we collectively composed a report that Miss Annie printed on the blackboard and we copied. I was selected as the person who would take our report, complete with sample seeds glued to it, and give it to Mr. Brown, our principal. I was honored. I practiced and practiced reading the report out loud until I almost knew it by heart. The reporting went well and Mr. Brown was very interested in our findings and thanked us for including him.

Aunt Gyp and Aunt Annie set up a reward system for grades. They would pay us $1.00 for each A on our report card. What a bonanza when the only thing I spent money on was a 10-cent movie and an occasional popcorn, Coca-Cola or ice cream cone at five cents. I do not remember spending my grade A money on anything. It went into my savings account at the bank until it was enough to buy a US Savings Bond. I had a little blue savings account book that I would take into the bank next door to Boo Collins' insurance office. Our banker, Mr. Johnson, usually came over to talk to me. The teller would record my deposit in the savings book. This went on for every report card at all grade levels. I always got all As.

For second grade, my teacher was Mrs. McCauley, who had the reputation of being stern and strict. I liked her a lot and thought she was fair. The highlight of that year for me was our Christmas play. During the course of the school year, each class was responsible for giving a program at the school assembly in the big auditorium. That year, our class was assigned the Christmas program.

Mrs. McCauley asked who wanted to be Santa Claus in the play. I raised my hand. Lots of the children laughed, but lo and behold, Mrs. McCauley chose me! This confirmed for me the Bible verse memorized at the previous summer's Bible School:

Ask, and it shall be given to you; seek, and ye shall find; knock, and it shall be opened to you. For every one who asketh receiveth; and he that seeketh findeth; and to him that knocketh, it shall be opened.

If you do not ask for what you want, if you do not try, you will never know what is possible.

In the play, I wore a Santa Claus suit and had a long white beard. We practiced the play and all the students had a part.

My mother said I was the star. I thought she meant because Santa Claus was the central character. However, she said I was the star because every time the audience would clap, laugh or otherwise react, I would turn completely around to face the audience with a big, broad, toothless smile!

Skippy and I—and lots of our friends—took piano lessons. Mrs. Lockhart was our teacher and every year we had a recital where each student played their best song. We all dressed in white and donned a cape to designate our group. Skippy's group wore red capes and my group, blue. I was not talented at playing the piano and I did not like to practice. I did enjoy learning about music. I especially enjoyed group lessons to study rhythm and play the rhythm band instruments.

We took a field trip to Raleigh to hear the North Carolina Symphony Orchestra. Mrs. Lockhart played records of the musical pieces the symphony would perform so we were familiar with the music before the trip. When we sat in the concert hall, hearing and actually feeling the music, it was utterly breathtaking. I could not have imagined anything so moving.

Third grade was difficult for me. My teacher was "Miss Mary Leigh" Webb. Miss Mary Leigh's husband was John Graham Webb, a cousin of my daddy's. We had often visited John Graham and Mary Leigh at their home and they visited us, too. Miss Mary Leigh was also a gardener and had a beautiful yard. At school, I was not allowed to call her Miss Mary Leigh and instead I had to call her Mrs. Webb. Mrs. Webb was strict, especially with me. However, after lunch every day she would read to us. She was an excellent read-aloud reader, like my mother.

When I was in third grade, Skippy was away at boarding school getting special classes for his dyslexia. That was the year Paul Cameron started school.

The only time I ever remember being in trouble at school happened in Mrs. Webb's class. One day, on our way back to class after recess, I saw Paul Cameron headed down the front steps, out of the school. I broke ranks to check on him. He was going home. He did not like school, so he was leaving. While I explained to him that he could not do that—that he had to go back to class—an angry and stern Mrs. Webb came out to get me and marched me back to class. I was in BIG trouble. I tried to explain, but she would not listen. Not only was I worried about being in trouble myself, I was worried about my little brother, who went on his merry way home!

Lots of people had stories about my little brother and they usually began something like this:

"Paul Cameron...Oh Lawdy, Paul Cameron..."

"Paul Cameron...Oh my goodness, they threw away the mold..."

"Paul Cameron...What's next?"

"Paul Cameron...What a character!"

"Character" in this context is defined as someone who is unique, eccentric. This fits my brother, Paul Cameron! He was bright, inquisitive and inventive. He certainly marched to the beat of a drummer heard by no one else; he listened not to the chords of convention; and he rode his pony and lived his young life with abandon.

Paul Cameron's best friend was Kaye Williams, my friend Sonny's little sister. Kaye was pretty and had long, thick, shiny brown pigtails. Paul Cameron always called her "Marion Kaye," her full double name. If we would call her Kaye, Paul Cameron would correct us: "Her name is Marion Kaye." He would jump on his pony, Smokey Joe, and ride down the hill to pick Kaye up for a ride. He usually rode bareback, and when Kaye would tell him she could not mount the pony he would say, "Marion Kaye, come here," and he would reach down, sweep her up behind him and off they would go.

Once, Marion Kaye and Paul Cameron had been exploring woods behind her house. Paul Cameron jumped across a little muddy rivulet. Kaye said she could not jump that far. "Don't worry, Marion Kaye," he said as he flung off his brand new winter coat and with a swirl, placed it in the mud for her to walk over without getting wet. It didn't work, but it was gallant.

There was the time Paul Cameron went courting. He told Marion Kaye he loved her and asked her to marry him. She adored him, so of course she said she would. He produced my mother's diamond engagement ring and gave it to her. Kaye was excited to show her beautiful ring to her mother, who right away told Kaye, "We have to go see Alice," and they took the ring to my mother.

Paul Cameron invited Marion Kaye to a St. Matthew's Church picnic at someone's home out in the country. "This was not a Methodist picnic," Kaye remembers. As people she did not know crowded noisily through the big kitchen, loading their plates with food and laughing and talking, Kaye began to cry. The ladies tried to comfort her. One woman sat her on a kitchen stool and asked her what she could get for her, "fried chicken…a ham sandwich…a piece of cake…." Soon, Paul Cameron came to Kaye's side and stated, "I know what you need, Marion Kaye. You need a 'mater sammich!'" Kaye stopped crying as the nice lady brought her a tomato sandwich. Kaye was not comforted by the food, but by her good friend, Paul Cameron.

"Paul Cameron…Oh Lawdy! He was playing with matches and set the Webb's yard on fire—the fire almost got to the house."

"Paul Cameron…they threw away the mold! I woke up in the middle of the night and through the bathroom window, I saw Paul Cameron riding Smokey Joe across our back yard."

"Paul Cameron… What's next? Did you hear the one about The Mystery at the Livery Stable?" There was a livery stable down at the bottom of Churton Street near the Eno River. One summer, when employees would arrive for work, one of the horses would be lathered and sweating. The vet was consulted. Then the owner staked out the stable overnight. Sure enough, in the early pre-dawn hours, Paul Cameron was caught breaking into the stable.

"Don't wrestle with ol' Hard Rock! Paul Cameron was wrestling with his daddy and broke his ribs."

In fourth grade, we discovered the world. We studied geography. The geography book was larger than our other books. It was square and had a faded mustard-yellow cover with black and white pictures inside. The first geography lesson was about the Fertile Crescent between the Tigris and Euphrates Rivers, said to be the birthplace of civilization, a place where writing, agriculture and astronomy began and where the wheel was first used. The book described irrigation systems devised centuries ago and the richness of the land and culture. There were maps of the region.

On the sidewalk between my house and school, I found cracks in the sidewalk that looked just like the Tigris and Euphrates River with the Fertile Crescent right there!

Our teacher, Mrs. Brown, was a Baptist. That year, the Baptist Church revival featured a missionary to Africa. Mrs. Brown invited the missionary to talk to our class about his work and life in Africa. It was truly interesting. He told us about the daily lives of the people he worked with, about the countryside, the trees, plants and animals. The world was huge, and we found out that we knew so little about it. I have had a keen interest in geography and love of it ever since fourth grade!

In the spring, my parents and my grandmother called Skippy, Paul Cameron and me to join them on the porch. There, they told us that mother was going to have a baby. We would have a baby brother or sister! I was so excited. I was sure it would be a sister! It would be only fair—two boys/two girls. Our Webb cousins had a baby brother, Billy. Billy was really cute and it was fun to play with him on the floor. However, I was convinced that a baby brother would be sort of like a puppy. He would be cute and cuddly only when he was a little baby.

Sure enough, on September 3, 1949, we had a baby girl—Margaret MacVicar Webb. The Margaret was because we had lots of Margarets in our family, including my great grandmother, Margaret Cameron Peebles. The MacVicar was for my living grandmother whose maiden name was MacVicar. We called little Margaret MacVicar "Peggy" because that is a nickname for Margaret. She was so tiny and adorable and we loved her to pieces!

North Carolina history starred in Miss Black's fifth-grade class. Again, the most fun was putting on our play for the school assembly. In this program, we demonstrated the Virginia Reel and other folk dances. We also played the Scotch-Irish music that settlers brought to our region.

We built our program on North Carolina history and featured how pioneers planted and harvested cotton, cleaned the seeds from it, spun it into thread at a spinning wheel, wove the thread into cloth and made clothes from the cloth. Such a lot of work just for something to wear!

This was particularly relevant to us because Hillsborough had two cotton mills that made cotton cloth a whole lot faster. I wondered why we never took a field trip to the cotton mills. I would have liked that.

A dance teacher from Durham offered dance lessons in Hillsborough. Once again, Skippy and I took lessons with our friends. We learned to tap dance. We learned folk dances like square dances and the Virginia Reel. My favorite was ballroom dancing, especially the waltzes. It became a lot more fun to waltz with a boy than to play football with him.

Because I could dance and because I was friends with ninth graders like my brother, I was invited to dances at the Craig's house. Mrs. Craig taught at the high school. Mr. and Mrs. Craig loved to dance and their house in the country sported a ballroom just for dancing. They would routinely invite students to their home for dances. Parents would take and pick up the students. Sometimes seniors could drive themselves.

When I was first invited and my parents decided that I could go, my mother made me an evening dress. It was a floor-length dress made of a pretty cotton flowered print. It was not to be confused with a dancing dress like Ginger Rogers wore in the movies, made of satin, silk or chiffon, and sprinkled with sparkles, but I thought it was beautiful and it did swirl when I waltzed.

Sixth grade was unique and I probably learned more that year than any other year because of challenges offered by being taught in unusual circumstances.

The Hillsborough school was too small. We did not have enough rooms for all the classes. In an educational innovation, the school took the top students in the sixth and seventh grades and set up a one-room class in a small brick building behind the Methodist Church, with both classes taught by a gifted teacher, Mrs. McBane. She would teach one class and make assignments then teach the other class. I was so lucky to be in that sixth grade class! My mind was absorbing all the lessons in both classes.

School was both interesting and fun, and I made so many friends at the little classroom and in high school. It was a great year, but it was to be my last in Hillsborough.

My parents had made the decision to buy a flower shop and move our family to my mother's home state of Florida over the Christmas break.

I was sad to leave my home, my friends, our extended family and our familiar and comfortable town, but my parents said I could come back in the summer and stay as long as I wanted to. My friends declared they would come to visit in Florida.

There was a big going-away party for us at the Moore's house; all our friends came. Dr. Moore, our dentist, and Mrs. Moore were friends of our parents. They had a son, Walton, who was Skip's age and a son, Billy Davis, who was my age. Mrs. Moore had bought a silver charm bracelet for our friends to give me. I thought it was a thoughtful and special gift. I appreciated it so very much and wore it to remember my home and friends.

When school let out for Christmas vacation, my parents loaded us in the station wagon, and we set out for Florida, driving all night with every radio station along the way playing "The Tennessee Waltz" sung by Patti Page. This was a sad song about lost love, but it was not as sad as I felt about my lost home, family, friends and familiar places. I tried to look forward:

Florida, land of sunshine

Florida, land of sandy beaches, blue lakes and silver springs

Florida, land of swamps, cypress trees with knees and mangrove trees that walk in water on stilts

Florida, land of palm trees, orange trees and sprawling live oaks, elegantly draped with Spanish moss

Florida, La Florída, land of flowers, awaited us with new adventures!

Behind the Scenes

In these stories, my parents were young—in their twenties and thirties. When I was born, my mother was twenty-four and my father twenty-eight. When we moved to Florida they were just thirty-five and thirty-nine. Both parents were intelligent, well-educated, artistic, creative, and fun-loving, but probably not the best equipped to deal with the emotional and financial hardships and struggles presented by their four children.

Neither of my parents had been raised in the typical early 20th century family with both a mother and father. My father's parents both died when he was twelve, and he and his sisters lived with their grandmother and attended boarding schools. My mother's father died when she was three; she and her younger sister were raised by their widowed mother, who worked as a nurse. My mother also attended boarding schools as a young girl.

Imagine the angst, frustration, suffering and financial ruin these young parents endured coping with their children's illnesses and conditions. Skippy's dyslexia required tutoring, private boarding school and special summer camps. My osteomylitis kept me in the hospital for weeks and months at a time, undergoing numerous surgeries and treatments over a four-year period.

Paul Cameron's eccentricity was sociopathic and never understood. Later, baby Margaret MacVicar was to be diagnosed with leukemia.

Behind the scenes of this happy childhood memoir, life was not so rosy—with depression, alcoholism, financial disaster and hopelessness playing key roles. Both sides of the family had supporting roles, providing money, childcare, clothes, emotional support and encouragement.

Why did we move to Florida? For financial reasons. We could not afford the house; we could not afford the lifestyle. Earlier, my father had moved the flower shop to our house; we had taken in a boarder; even we children had cashed our saving bonds.

Florida offered a new business, a smaller house, fewer expenses, a fresh start.

Family Homes and Familiar Places in the 21st Century

The spelling of Hillsborough has reverted to its original spelling, Hillsborough.

Cousin Mary and Cousin Paul Collins' home, Highlands, is still in the family, occupied by their granddaughter, Elizabeth W. Goode, and her family.

My Aunt Eliza's house, Bellevue, was for a time a bed and breakfast called Hillsborough House, but currently is a private residence.

The Kirkland home, Ayr Mount, passed from family ownership after four generations, upon the death of Samuel Kirkland in 1971. In 1984, a nephew of Sam's widow sold it to Richard Hampton Jenrette, who restored the house and lands and added Ayr Mount to the Classical American Homes Preservation Trust. Ayr Mount is open to the public. http://www.classicalamerican.org/html/ayrmount_history.html

Stagville, located in Durham County, is one of the Bennehan-Cameron plantations and is operated by North Carolina Historic Homes, NC Division of Cultural Resources as Historic Stagville. Visitors can tour the Bennehan home, rare two-story slave houses, a huge barn and the cemetery. http://www.stagville.org/

Fairntosh, another of the Bennehan-Cameron plantations, near Stagville in Durham County is privately owned and is operated as an equestrian center and bed and breakfast. http://www.fairntosh.com/

Burnside, home of Paul Carrington Cameron, site where the Regulators were hanged prior to the Revolutionary War and the site of Thomas Ruffin's Law Office, is a private residence.

The Ruffin-Roulhac House has been restored and serves as the Hillsborough Town Hall. It is, of course, open to the public. http://www.historichillsborough.org/content/ruffin-roulhac-house-0

The building that housed The Corner Drug Store and my daddy's flower shop is now a popular restaurant.

What was our 1940s public library with the cool floors, once known as the Confederate Memorial Library, is now home to the Orange County Historical Museum. http://www.orangenchistory.org/

The historic Colonial Inn on West King Street, a popular inn and dining venue since the mid-18th century, stands crumbling in place in a most dilapidated state.

The Orange County Court House is still the town-center and its clock continues to mark the hours as it has now for centuries.

The churches where I went to Sunday School and Bible School look much the same as they did in the 1940s.

St. Matthew's congregation is much larger and Sunday School classes are now taught in a fine parish house named for Thomas Ruffin. Thomas Ruffin had given the land for St. Matthew's, the spot where he proposed to Anne Kirkland.

St. Matthew's cemetery is a final resting place for many more of my family now. Late on a recent summer afternoon, my daughter and I visited, shared a cocktail and memories with them.

Warm Firesides Wide Porches

To learn more about the people and places in the authentic southern town of Hillsborough North Carolina go to http://www.visithillsboroughnc.com/

NOTE: Our house, the Thomas Norfleet Webb House, burned down in 1951 after our family had moved to Florida. The magnolia tree there still looks inviting.

Sally Ann Webb McPherson

My Forefathers

James Hogg

James Hogg (1729-1804) emigrated from Scotland, bringing an expedition of 280 Scot Highlanders with him aboard his ship, the Bachelor.

He first went to Wilmington, NC, where his brother was a successful merchant. Later he moved his family to Hillsborough, where he met Richard Henderson, a judge and chief organizer of the western land speculation known as the Transylvania Company. The company had contracted with Daniel Boone to blaze a trail across Cumberland Gap into Kentucky and negotiate with the Indians to buy land to form a new colony, Transylvania. In November 1775, James Hogg journeyed to Philadelphia to negotiate with members of the Continental Congress, among them Samuel Adams, John Adams, and Thomas Jefferson, over admission of Transylvania as a fourteenth colony. The Congress would not act without the consent of North Carolina and Virginia. The claims of the Transylvania Company were never recognized.

As a trustee of the University of North Carolina from 1789 to 1802, James Hogg exerted strong influence in favor of Chapel Hill as the location for the school.

James Hogg, concerned that his children not be burdened by his surname, petitioned the General Assembly to change the name of his male heirs to their mother's last name, Huske. This gave rise to the rhyme, "Hogg by name, hog by nature, changed to Huske by the legislature."

James' granddaughter, Anne Alves Huske, married Dr. James Webb, MD.

Warm Firesides Wide Porches

The Transylvania Expedition, led by Daniel Boone,
left from this spot in Hillsborough, North Carolina
to explore the land beyond the mountains. The plaque is inscribed,
"And they marched away solemnly as if going to the ends of the world."

Sally Ann Webb McPherson

Dr. James Webb, M.D.

Dr. James Webb (1774-1855) was the son of William Webb, born Feb. 20, 1774, in Granville County, North Carolina. He attended the University of North Carolina and studied medicine at the University of Pennsylvania's Jefferson Medical College.

He was a noted physician, merchant and banker, residing in Hillsborough NC. He married Anne Alves Huske, daughter of John Huske and granddaughter of James Hogg. They had ten children.

Dr. Webb was a founder and the first Vice President of the North Carolina Medical Society of 1799. Under his leadership the Medical Society developed a Board of Censors that led to the formation of the Board of Medical Examiners in 1859. North Carolina was the first state in the Union to enact such laws. In 1849, the medical society, which had not met for years, was replaced by the Medical Society of the State of North Carolina. Dr. Webb was the only founding member of both.

Dr. James Webb, MD took the groundbreaking step of providing free smallpox vaccinations, and he also provided free care to poor white and black patients.

Dr. Webb was a trustee of the University of North Carolina.

Dr. Webb's son, James (1816-1897) married Sarah Frances Cheshire. Their son, Joseph Cheshire Webb, married Mary Alice Hill. They were my great grandparents.

William Kirkland

William Kirkland (1768-1836) was born in Scotland. By 1792, he settled comfortably in Hillsborough as a successful merchant and planter. He married Margaret Bain Scott and they had fourteen children.

He built a family home, Ayr Mount, on a large tract of land along the Eno River in 1815. Ayr Mount remained in the family for four generations, until 1985. It was purchased by Richard Hampton Jenrette, who meticulously researched and restored the home and grounds.

One of William and Margaret Kirkland's daughters, Anne, married Thomas Ruffin.

Sally Ann Webb McPherson

Thomas Ruffin

Thomas Carter Ruffin (1787-1870) was born in Virginia, the son of a Methodist minister. He moved to North Carolina as a child. He graduated college from the University of New Jersey, later Princeton University. He studied law with Archibald DeBow Murphy and was admitted to the North Carolina bar. He settled in Hillsborough in 1808.

Thomas Ruffin married William Kirkland's beautiful daughter, Anne, when she was fifteen years old. They had fourteen children.

Ruffin had a very lucrative law practice and twice served as Chief Justice of the Supreme Court of North Carolina, writing landmark opinions that are still studied in the 21st century. Before the Civil War, he opposed succession and attended the Peace Conference in Washington, D.C. in 1861. However, he defended the South's right to secede and later supported the war. After the war, he petitioned for a pardon from President Johnson and received one.

In addition to legal and political careers, Ruffin was a farmer with plantations in Alamance and Rockingham Counties; he was president of the state's Agricultural Society. He was also a banker.

He was a Trustee of the University of North Carolina for twenty-three years.

His son, Thomas Ruffin Jr., was also a Supreme Court Justice. His daughter, Anne, married Paul Carrington Cameron; his granddaughter, Margaret Cameron was my great grandmother.

Richard Bennehan

Richard Bennehan (1743-1825), successful merchant and planter, came to Hillsborough from Virginia in 1768. He owned Snow Hill Plantation and he built Stagville Plantation in Durham County in 1787. He married Mary Armis, who had inherited vast land holdings upon the death of her father, Thomas Armis. Mary and Richard Bennehan had two children, Rebecca and Dudley. Rebecca married Duncan Cameron. Dudley never married.

Richard Bennehan was active in the founding of the University of North Carolina and served on the Board of Trustees.

Sally Ann Webb McPherson

Dr. Edmund Strudwick

Upon the death of his father, William Strudwick, in 1810, Edmund Strudwick at age eight became the ward of Dr. James Webb, MD of Hillsborough.

Edmund Strudwick (1802-1879) was a physician, a member of the U.S. House of Representatives and later, the North Carolina House of Representatives. He graduated from the University of Pennsylvania Medical School.

In 1849, Dr. Strudwick became the first elected president of the newly formed Medical Society of the State of North Carolina. During his presidency he helped implement "stiff requirements in general education and moral character for those seeking entrance into medical schools." He also pushed the legislature to pass a law compelling the registration of marriages, births, and deaths. He also stressed the importance of autopsies for educational purposes.

As the Civil War raged in 1862, Strudwick cared for the wounded in his own home. By the end of the war, his large estate had diminished to nothing. He surrendered all of his possessions and worked for the rest of his life to pay off his debts.

Dr. Strudwick was the grandfather of Sheppard Strudwick, Sr., who was president of the Bellevue Cotton Mill in Hillsborough and who carved the cross in the Hillsborough Presbyterian Church. Dr. Strudwick was the great grandfather of award-winning actor, Sheppard Strudwick, Jr. and renowned portrait artists Clement and Edmund Strudwick.

My Uncle Doc and his son, Verne Strudwick Caviness, Sr. and Jr., were named for Dr. Edmund Strudwick.

Duncan Cameron

Duncan Cameron (1777-1843) was the son of the Reverend John Cameron and Anne Owens Nash. John was an Anglican clergyman who came to America in 1770. He also ran a series of respected schools in the colonies.

Duncan Cameron was a successful attorney in Virginia who studied law under the renowned Paul Carrington of that state. He moved to Hillsborough in 1796 and married Rebecca Bennehan, daughter of Richard and Mary Bennehan. They had eight children, six girls and two sons, including Paul Carrington Cameron. In 1807, they moved to Stagville Plantation, and Duncan managed the combined Bennehan-Cameron lands. He built Fairntosh Plantation in Durham County.

Duncan also ran mercantile businesses and mills. He served as a Superior Court Judge and was a banker.

He was a Trustee of the University of North Carolina.

Paul Carrington Cameron

Paul Carrington Cameron (1808-1891), son of Duncan Cameron, married Anne Ruffin, daughter of Thomas Ruffin; they had ten surviving children. Paul was also an attorney, but his interest and talent was in agriculture and business. As the sole heir of Duncan Cameron, he inherited all the Bennehan and Cameron lands in North Carolina and added holdings in Alabama, Mississippi and Florida. Before and after the Civil War, Paul Carrington Cameron was the largest landowner in the south.

Paul Cameron built Burnside, the family home in Hillsborough and the small Law Office for his father-in-law, Thomas Ruffin, on the same property.

He was a Trustee of the University of North Carolina and is credited with the survival of the University after the Civil War.

Robert Bruce Peebles

Robert Bruce Peebles (1840-1916 was not from Hillsborough—he was from Jackson in North Hampton County in eastern North Carolina. He was an outdoorsman, excelling in hunting and fishing. During the Civil War, he left his studies at the University of North Carolina to enlist in the Confederate Army, where his bravery and leadership were highly praised. He received a battlefield promotion to adjutant-general. After the war, he returned to his studies; he was a successful lawyer and a Superior Court Judge for 14 years. His wife, my great grandmother, was Margaret Cameron Peebles, daughter of Paul Carrington Cameron.